VERMONT
BOOK
OF THE
DEAD

GRAVEYARD LEGENDS AND LORE

Roxie J. Zwicker

THE
History
PRESS

Published by The History Press
Charleston, SC
www.historypress.com

All images are courtesy of the author's collection.

First published 2023

Manufactured in the United States

ISBN 9781467155144

Library of Congress Control Number: 2023937209

*Vermont is a state that I love. I could not look upon the peaks of Ascutney,
Whittier, and Mansfield without being moved in a way that no other scene
could move me. It was here that I first saw the light of day; here that I received
my bride. Here my dead lie buried, pillowed among the everlasting hills. I love
Vermont because of her hills and valleys, her scenery and invigorating climate,
but most of all I love her because of her indomitable people. They are a race of
pioneers who almost impoverished themselves for love of others.
If ever the spirit of liberty should vanish from the rest of the Union,
it could all be restored by the generous store held by the people of this brave little
state of Vermont.*

*—excerpt from "Vermont Is a State I Love," President Calvin Coolidge,
September 19, 1928*

CONTENTS

INTRODUCTION

I have vivid memories of Vermont going back to my childhood, as it was only a short drive up Route 91 to the state from where I grew up in western Massachusetts. If I were to sum up the way I feel when visiting the state, I would say it is a peaceful feeling, a truly soul-stirring sensation that stays with you forever. The images in my mind of explorations through the hills and valleys are like surreal postcards of places I'd like to travel to again, perhaps to see if they are truly as spectacular as my memory serves me. It was always a sensory experience in Vermont, where there were layers to each visit and each step taken.

The golden leaves were glowing an electric yellow the day I drove through Smugglers Notch in Stowe. The road, which was once a traders' path that became a road in the nineteenth century, twists and turns around thousand-foot-tall cliffs and giant boulders that block the view ahead. My imagination ran wild with the stories of smugglers who traded everything from rum to all sorts of goods from places around the world, including Europe and the Caribbean. It's an ideal place to hide out, with hidden corners and secret caves blending into the dramatic scenery. There was a story of revenuers who were tracking smugglers to a cave when they decided to blow up the entrance with a barrel of gunpowder. A large portion of the mountainside came crashing down, and the smugglers are said to have been buried behind the rubble. Local legends tell us that their unhappy spirits may still haunt the notch.

One Vermont visit took me to the tiny town of Sandgate, just outside of Arlington. I was quite surprised to see that this tiny town of about 350 people was at the end of a dirt road. The West Cemetery in town dated to the 1790s, and I was quite excited to see it as I drove up the hill and

The lifelike sculpture of a harpist can be found on the grave of Edith R. Barry in Brookfield, Vermont.

parked in the grass. As soon as I opened the door of my car, I heard a hawk screeching overhead, and I looked up to see him flying about twenty feet above me. I stepped onto what looked like an old carriage path, and just a few steps along, a black racer snake crossed in front of me. As I watched him disappear into the tall grass, he looked to be at least three feet long. While the hawk continued to loudly make his presence known, I noticed two more snakes in the burial ground, and they were wrapped around the base of the warm marble gravestones. I must admit, nature almost got the best of me, as I was ready to go dashing back to the car. However, the allure of the old gravestones and their carvings kept my attention longer than I intended.

Every time I visit the Old Bennington Cemetery, reported to be the oldest burial ground in Vermont, I marvel at the intricate stone carvings I find there—in fact, I sometimes even gasp out loud. Some of what I consider to

The replacement gravestone for Justin Morgan, the man to whom the breed of the Morgan Horse is credited to.

be the most beautiful gravestones in all of New England can be found here. The picturesque church and long white fence frame the cemetery like an artist's canvas. I often think of how stunning a spot this is to be buried in, overlooking the scenic town below. It's almost as if those buried here don't have to go far to keep an eye on the future evolution of the settlement.

During one Vermont visit, I found myself on the trail of Justin Morgan, who is buried at the Randolph Center Cemetery. He was a talented musician, tavern keeper and famed horse breeder originally from western Massachusetts. The legendary lineage and intrigue of the Morgan horse eventually extended around the world, and the horse is the official animal of Vermont. Justin died at the age of fifty-one in 1798 from consumption, and there are several monuments, memorials and markers throughout the state that honor his contributions to history.

Some explorations through Vermont yielded a variety of weather experiences; sometimes, it seemed like all four seasons rumbled through in one day. Watching the light change over the old gravestones in the cemeteries was almost ethereal and, at moments, seemed just heavenly. As you turn the pages

The statue of Vermont's state animal the Morgan horse can be found at the University of Vermont Morgan Horse Farm in Weybridge.

of this book and explore these hallowed places with me, imagine the adventures I made to discover the stories and the stones. Red, vibrant covered bridges, sparkling streams, quaint hillside farms filled with cows, fields of wildflowers bent toward the sun and cemeteries seen and unseen between them all. While some areas of the state have seen growth and change, it is easy to find vast spaces that look exactly like they did two hundred years ago. Vermont has the second smallest population of any state, yet there are so many intriguing stories of people who were true individualists here. The people you are about to meet in these sacred places will tell us of their remarkable lives, memories and connections to the land. Which story will you find unforgettable?

1

DISCOVERING HISTORIC VERMONT GRAVEYARDS

Continuing our route along the west side of the lake, contemplating the country,
I saw on the east side, very high mountains, capped with snow. I asked the
Indians if those parts were inhabited. They answered me yes, and that they were
Iroquois, and there were in those parts, beautiful valleys and fields fertile in corn
as good as any I had eaten in the country, with an infinitude of other fruits,
and that the lake extended close to the mountains, which were according to my
judgment fifteen leagues from us.

—extract from Samuel de Champlain's narrative, 1609

There is evidence of Native occupation on the lands we now know as Vermont dating back thirteen thousand years. This evidence of the earliest people has been found in archaeological excavations. The pathway through the mountain ranges leading to the valleys were believed to have been taken by Paleo-Indian groups. Many Paleo-Indian sites have been found in the Champlain Basin. While ancient artifacts have been found here, human remains that predate the arrival of European explorers are extremely rare to find. The rich soil of the land has transformed those burial sites. In addition, sensitivity toward these sacred burial sites and the respect they require helps preserve the legacy of the area's past.

On the morning of July 4, 1609, French explorer Samuel de Champlain and his companions glided into the waters of the lake that eventually bore his name. In the years that followed, French military settlements were established and abandoned. The Massachusetts colony pushed north in the early eighteenth century. As the days of the American Revolution drew close, colonists from surrounding areas moved into the Vermont Territory. From 1749 to 1764, Vermont was part of New Hampshire, and then, in 1764, it became part of New York. In 1791, Vermont became an independent state and was the first to enter the Union after the original thirteen states.

The Bennington Center Cemetery is one of the oldest burial grounds in Vermont. The Old First Church was gathered on December 3, 1762, by separatists who had been influenced by the Great Awakening. The oldest gravestone there dates to 1762. Places to bury the dead were established on homesteads, next to churches and in town centers almost as quickly as the settlements themselves.

Some family burial grounds later expanded to become larger cemeteries for the community. One of the first settlers of the town of West Barnet, Vermont, was Claudius Stuart, who arrived from Scotland around 1775. The story was that one day, his wife was gathering brush on a hill when she said that when she died, she wanted to be buried on that spot. As requested, she was buried there when she died in 1781. Just twenty years later, she was joined by her two sons, James and William, who had drowned while attempting to cross the Connecticut River in a boat. Claudius died in 1811, and this space remained a family burial ground cared for by the family until the death of William Stuart in 1879. Charles, whose son lived in Illinois, offered to donate the land and as much adjoining property as needed to build a village burial ground to Barnet. It was also documented in Barnet that there was a county burial place that was established near the Danville line that contained thirty graves. The establishment of Memorial Day at the close of the Civil War helped develop a "kindlier sentiment" toward the final resting places of the dead, according to town history books.

According to the town history of Newbury, as of 1785, "the town purchased a 'burying cloth' in accordance with the usage of the time." This cloth was made of heavy black material, had a gilt fringe and tassels and was large enough to cover the coffin while it was being borne to the grave on a bier. The burying cloth was owned by the town, and a small fee was charged for its use. In these early days, coffins were not bought ready-made but were ordered by the local carpenter when needed. It was not uncommon in many places—although it was perhaps uncommon in Newbury—for people of some wealth to have their coffins made while they

Several burial sites in Vermont have been moved over the years, including these graves in Sharon.

were still living. And in these cases, considerable expense was sometimes lavished. The custom, now universal, of enclosing a coffin in an outer box for burial, came about during the Civil War, although it was occasionally observed before.

As the folk of Vermont got to know the land, discoveries of burial grounds that predated the early colonists were made. In 1873 the discovery of an ancient burial ground was described in the *History of Vermont* by Edward Day Collins written in 1903:

> *About two miles north of the village of Swanton in northwestern Vermont, is a sandy ridge, which was formally covered by a dense growth of Norway Pines; the thickly set, straight trees resembling somewhat a huge growth of hemp. The place was at one time called "the old hemp yard," a name which still clings to it. Rather more than twelve years ago it was discovered that beneath as forest stone implements were buried, and further investigation has shown that the spot, which was so covered with large trees and stumps when the first white men first came into the region*

Left: The gravestone for Lucy Ann Bayley at the Oxbow Cemetery in Newbury depicts a clipped rose to symbolize a life that has ended.

Right: A hand plucks a flower on the grave of Martha Bayley, who was twenty-three when she died in 1858, at the Oxbow Cemetery in Newbury.

had been ages before, used as a burial place by some people whose only records are the various objects which the affectionate care of the living placed in the graves of the dead. From directly beneath the largest trees, or half-decayed stumps some of these relics were taken, so we may feel sure that before the great pines which for many years, perhaps centuries, grew, flourished, and decayed, had germinated, these graves were dug, and with unknown ceremonies, the bodies of the dead were placed in them, together with those articles that had been used during life, or were supposed to be needed in a future existence. We cannot know how many successive growths of trees may have followed each other since the forest began to usurp the place set apart for sepulture.

Remarkably, many of the gravestones in Vermont endure because of the strength of the stone they were carved from. Quarried from deep within the earth, the finest Vermont marble, slate and granite were carved to share the artistry, iconography and stories of those buried here. In reading these chiseled words, we will discover, in some cases, the joy of living in Vermont in its early days, while some carvings tell us of the tragedies and dangers the first settlers endured. The burial places of Vermont each share in the telling of the history of Vermont from its earliest settlements through the battles and skirmishes bravely fought to establish a thriving state that is rich in beauty and history.

2

SOUTHERN VERMONT

DORSET, VERMONT

The depths of the mountains in Dorset, Vermont, reveal the geology and rich roots of the mountain range. The area's three rivers, meandering brooks and active ponds offer opportunities to connect to the scenic vistas of the town. In 2017, Dorset was named the most beautiful town in Vermont by a travel media company.

The Maple Hill Cemetery was established in 1772 and is still being used today. A variety of storied Vermonters sleep peacefully here. Elizabeth Payson Prentiss was a pastor's wife who wrote twenty-five books, mostly centering on juvenile and religious fiction. Described as a compassionate woman who gave comfort to those in need, she lost two of her children in the span of three months: her son Edward at the age of four and newborn daughter Bessie. She wrote of her sorrow:

"My Nursery," 1852

I thought that prattling boys and girls Would fill this empty room;
That my rich heart would gather flowers From childhood's opening bloom.
One child and two green graves are mine, This is God's gift to me;
A bleeding, fainting, broken heart—
This is My gift to thee.

The white marble gravestone marking Elizabeth and her husband, Reverend George's, grave resides in the shade of young trees. Delicately carved flowers and ferns eternally bloom within a never-ending circle.

A simple, white marble gravestone stands on the grave of famed painters Reginald and Felicia Marsh. Reginald was born in Paris, France, and graduated from Yale University in 1920. His innovative style of painting influenced many artists. His subject matter of New York City street life remains popular with famous galleries and fine art collectors. He was a summer resident of Dorset and died of a heart attack at the age of fifty-six on July 3, 1954.

Also in the cemetery is the grave of respected elder Jonathan Roberts, who was a successful farmer and lifelong resident of Dorset. While he was having a conversation with two other townsfolk, he fell over and died on December 12, 1911. He was buried next to his wife of sixty years, who had died earlier the same year.

The first commercial marble quarry in America was established in Dorset in 1785, just twenty-four years after the town was chartered in 1761. Dorset marble has distinctive green and blue accents and streaks and has been used to build mansions on Fifth Avenue in New York and numerous

Giant slabs of marble surround the historic marker for the first marble quarry in the United States that started in Dorset, Vermont, in 1785.

historic buildings as far away as Washington, D.C., and Montreal, Canada. Headstones carved out of Dorset marble can be found all over Vermont. Over five thousand gravestones from the appropriately named Gettysburg Quarry now stand on Civil War battlefields, etched with names and dates that shouldn't be forgotten.

Today, there are many abandoned quarries in Dorset, and some have hiking trails that visitors can use to explore the area. Pools of turquoise waters surrounded by walls of marble can be found in and around the mountains. A sharp eye can discover abandoned quarrying equipment and a variety of stone cellar holes that were part of houses lived in by migrant quarry workers. Mount Aeolus supplied fine marble for gravestones and building materials for well over one hundred years. Curiously, the caves found in the mountain were once home to the Northeast's largest bat population. Bats would travel up to 170 miles to drop down into the caverns to sleep "the sleep of near death" until the spring, when the caverns were said to "breathe." By the early 2000s, white nose syndrome had killed nearly 90 percent of the bat population in these caves. The bones that litter the caves' floors today greatly outnumber the small groups of bats that still gather in the mountains. Dorset, Vermont, has a deep history that stirs in its mountains and is remembered in its graveyards.

ROCKINGHAM MEETING HOUSE CEMETERY

Rockingham, Vermont

A small, weathered green sign stands at the end of the hillside roadway to the Rockingham Meeting House, welcoming visitors to this National Historic Landmark. Tucked underneath the hill is the old receiving tomb, which would have been used for cold storage during the winter months for the graveyard next to the meetinghouse. Because the ground would freeze in the winter, burials could not be conducted, so the bodies would be stored in the tomb. In the spring, when the ground thawed, the bodies could be properly interred. There are a handful of receiving tombs in New England that are still being used for this purpose.

It was 1752 when New Hampshire governor Benning Wentworth granted a plot of land to a group of gentlemen farmers from western Massachusetts, which later became known as Rockingham, Vermont. After the French and

The town tomb is viewable from the roadside, just beneath the meetinghouse.

Indian War ended in 1761, many people moved from the Upper Connecticut River Valley to settle in the area. The plans to build the current meetinghouse were approved by the town in 1787. The director of the project was master builder General John Fuller, who lived about a mile away from the site.

When the community came together to build the meetinghouse, there was a dramatic moment that was recalled in a letter from an aged man in the nineteenth century: "After he got everything ready the old General took a bottle of rum in one hand, a tumbler in the other and stood on the plate of the bent on the south side, then he gave the order to put it up in that position. He rode up on the plate, and he was a man weighing 200 pounds. When they had got it up he stood on the plate, drank his health to the crowd below, then threw his bottle and tumbler down and called for the ladder, coming down amid long and loud cheering."

The meetinghouse has many stories to tell, from that of the drawing of a man dressed in a colonial outfit (complete with a powdered wig) on the wall to those about the numerous wooden box pews and the elevated pulpit with the original soundboard behind it. The meetinghouse was never heated, which brings to mind the day-long sermons that would have required families to gather closely together underneath handmade quilts and blankets to stay warm. The meetinghouse saw an extensive renovation in 1906. In 1932, the *Vermont Phoenix* newspaper reported on the twenty-sixth annual pilgrimage to the meetinghouse, where one thousand people were in attendance on a dark and dreary day. Judge Rowland Davis of the New York Supreme Court gave the address that afternoon: "My presence here today is, I think, due more to ancestry than to my own merits. Nathaniel Davis, my great-great-grandfather, was one of the founders of this church and one of the four men who granted land on which this building was erected, and the lands of the adjoining burying ground, in which he and at least two of his sons now lie sleeping."

The curiosity about this enduring structure continues to this day. In 2021, an examination of paint chip samples by a conservator suggests that the meetinghouse was most likely painted dark red, not white, as it is today. The meetinghouse is open for tours in the summer and the early fall. Standing inside the meetinghouse, the view of the burial ground

Memento mortis means "remember death." Early gravestones were often grim reminders of death.

through the large windows is compelling and helps bring visitors back in time. You can almost hear the sermons of Reverend Samuel Whiting, the first minister at the meetinghouse who served thirty-six years at the pulpit. He died in 1819 and was buried in the yard behind the building under a marble gravestone.

The earliest burials here date to the 1770s, and there are a fair amount of significant, historic gravestone carvings to be found. A style from what is known as the Rockingham school of stone carving can be found here. Moses Wright came up from Northfield, Massachusetts, along with his son and son-in-law, as a farmer and stone-carver. It is believed that Moses learned the trade from the "Westminster Master" from nearby Westminster, Vermont, but their name has been lost to time. The carver would use a steel compass to draw a circle on the stone and then carve the image and stylized details into the stone.

A fine example of a Wright-carved stone is the gravestone of Artamus Aldrich. A floating head underneath an arch, with detailed eyelashes and wavy hair, is carved into the center of the stone. Small hearts, daisy wheels/hex signs and vines can be found carved on the borders of the stone. The inscription for this Revolutionary War hero is particularly interesting:

SACRED
to the Memory of the
Elder Artamus Aldrich Who Was found Dead under his Grist Mill wheel
Feb. 9th, 1796 In the 50th year of his age.

There are also several stones with sun face carvings, including one stone with three suns on it for Betty Lane and her twins. The carvings represent hopeful souls before God on Judgement Day.

Sacred to the memory of Mrs. Betty Lane who died June 22, 1791 in the
34th year of her
age and also her twins, one stillborn the others age 3 days.
Our flesh shall slumber in the ground,
Till the last trumpets joyfull sound.
Then burst the chains with sweet surprize, And in our Saviour's image rise.

The small gravestone for the infant Bellows twins, a girl and a boy who died in 1799, is of particular interest, as the gravestone was removed and put on display at the Brooklyn Museum of Art in 1963 for an exhibition

Left: Three solemn-looking suns are carved into the gravestone of Betty Lane and her twin children.

Right: Elder Artamus Aldrich was found dead under his gristmill wheel.

on the folk art style of New England gravestone carvings. To see the tiny details of the carving, one must get quite close to it. The carving is of two wide-eyed children in their crib underneath a quilt. The inscription reads, "Sleep on sweet babes & take your rest / God called you home he thought it best."

A white marble gravestone for Emily Rice can be found with rusted metal braces holding it together. Emily was the wife of Levi Rice, and according to the stone's inscription, she died at the age of twenty-two years, seven months and nineteen days in 1837. There was a belief in being very specific about the age of a person on their gravestone, as it would serve as a reminder to cherish every moment of every day. The carving depicts a flowy curtain pulled back to reveal a blooming flower; however, a careful study of the stone reveals a carved cut tulip lying on its side at the bottom of the stone to represent a life cut short.

Nearby is the grave of Melissa Rice, who was the wife of another Levi Rice, who died in 1888 at the age of forty-nine years, four months and twenty-two days. Her gravestone depicts cat tails and eternal flame lamps along its borders. The inscription tells us that she "passed to the higher life."

Right: The Bellows infants' gravestone has a carving depicting two infants in their crib underneath a quilt.

Below: This empty bed sculpture is meant to appear like it once held a sleeping child who was just called away.

Above: Looking across the Meetinghouse Cemetery in Rockingham, Vermont.

Opposite: This antique hearse in Rockingham is in remarkable condition for its age.

The base of the stone is cracked in several places and shows signs of repairs made over the years.

A small carved stone bed, complete with a fluffed pillow and fringed blanket cast aside, can be found in one of the cemetery rows. It appears as if someone has just climbed out of the bed and walked away, perhaps, in this case, to go to heaven. The attention to detail here is extraordinary for this Victorian-era memorial.

The gravestone of William Stearns Jr., who died "by the means of a fall in his tenth year," explains: "Altho my days are short and few, I've finished what I had to do. And now my Jesus bids me come. I thus obey him and go home." The face carved at the center of the stone has a slightly downturned mouth, perhaps suggesting the sadness of the occasion.

Willow trees, stars and leafy vines can be discerned on early nineteenth-century gravestones. A figure with a furrowed brow, carved with several lines on its face, can be found on the grave of John Felt, who was twenty-three when he died in 1805. Some gravestones that have been thrust out of the ground show their carver's signatures, such as "Made By M. Wright."

The grave for Josiah White, who, according to his gravestone, died at the age of ninety-six in 1806, tells of the legacy that this man left behind. "The descendants of Josiah White at his death. Children 15 - Grandchildren 160 - Great Grandchildren 211 - Children deceased 2 - Grandchildren 26 - Great Grandchildren 35."

Tucked away inside the 1849 hearse barn at the edge of the graveyard is the 1816 hearse that was built by E.P. Osgood of Saxtons River, Vermont. The hearse is still in relatively good shape, considering its age, and it still has its ivory tassel curtains hanging in its windows. Underneath the boards of the hearse are tiny drilled holes that sharp screws would have poked through to help hold the coffins securely in place as they were carried up and down the hills and lanes of Vermont on the way to their burial places.

IMMANUEL CEMETERY

Bellows Falls

The story of the mistress of finance Hetty Green is one of a headstrong and ambitious woman. How Hetty earned the "Witch of Wall Street" moniker has deep roots in New England history. She was descended from John Howland, one of 102 Puritan passengers on the *Mayflower*. Hetty was born in the town of New Bedford, Massachusetts, which had been named by John after his hometown of Bedford, England. The family had amassed quite a bit of wealth through generations in the whaling industry and the shipping trade with China.

Hetty went to a Quaker school on Cape Cod and then went to a seminary in Boston. Her father, Edward, had her read financial papers and books to him; he died in 1865, when Hetty was just thirty years old, leaving her millions of dollars. Hetty had some involvement with the New York socialite society, but she did this on her own terms and in her own way. Instead of having a fine apartment in the city, she stayed in a boardinghouse. When she went to parties, rather than pay for cab fare, she would put heavy wool stockings on over her shoes and walk through the snow, just to save a little money.

When Hetty's aunt Sylvia Ann Howland died, a court battle ensued over the inheritance. Hetty declared that her aunt had told her the money was hers when she died. The case was dismissed on a technicality, but Hetty appealed it to the United States Supreme Court, and she received a substantial settlement. From that point on, for most of Hetty's life, some sort of legal battle was going on, whether it was a lawsuit or a financial issue with her lawyers. She was so angered by the constant legal issues that she said, "I would rather have my daughter burned at the stake than to go through what I have with lawyers."

In 1867, she married Edward H. Green, who had made a fortune in the silk and tea trade. Right before they married, Hetty had an agreement drawn up that no matter what debts her husband incurred, her fortune was to remain solely hers. Edward lived a more lavish lifestyle and wasn't as focused on finances as she was. In a bold move that surprised many people, Hetty later took her children and walked out on her husband. Years later, her daughter Sylvia was married, and her son Edward "Ned" became a business tycoon in his own right.

Hetty had developed quite a reputation for the eccentric way she did business. On one occasion, she needed to travel from Philadelphia to New York before the close of business, and she stood to make thousands on the deal. The railroad company quoted her for the trip with the engine and one car. She told the company to take the car off so the trip would cost five dollars less; she would ride in the locomotive cab. The deal was made, and she made it to Wall Street in time.

She wore mostly black and a little bonnet, and she wouldn't ride in a carriage. Nor was she ever seen at the theater or the opera. She never disclosed the secrets of her success, and when asked what was good to invest in, her answer was usually "the other world." She invested in real estate and knew how to buy low and sell high. Through her shrewd business sense and attention to detail, she had become the richest woman in America. Her Quaker upbringing was a foundation for some of the choices that she made. She loaned money to churches, secretly gave gifts to charitable causes and helped support a number of struggling families.

Hetty lived between New York and Bellows Falls, Vermont, and she usually traveled alone on business trips, which was unheard of for women at the time. Eventually, she took her husband back, and they lived in the house in Bellows Falls, where he died in 1902. Hetty then converted to the Episcopalian faith so she could be buried next to him in the Immanuel Episcopal Church Cemetery in Bellows Falls. Hetty died on July 3, 1916, and newspapers across the globe printed the news: the "Witch of Wall Street was dead." A tall yet modest obelisk marks the grave of Hetty and her husband. The graves for Annetti's children, Ned and Sylvia, can also be found in the cemetery. Ned lived quite comfortably and married

The modest obelisk for Hetty Green, the "Witch of Wall Street."

an alleged prostitute whom his mother didn't approve of. Sylvia married into the famous Astor family when she married a man twenty-five years her senior. When she died, she left $90 million, nearly her entire fortune, to charities, churches and hospitals. The house that Hetty Green lived in on the corner of Church and Westminster Streets in Bellows Falls was torn down. The staircase and a few architectural pieces were salvaged and used in other area homes. For a short time, a park stood on the site. Today, in an ironic twist, much of that park is now the location of a bank, an interesting chapter for the location that was once home of the wealthiest woman in America.

Burgess Cemetery

Grafton

I had traveled several times through the picturesque and idyllic village of Grafton on a rainy day, looking for a particular gravestone. I passed the historic Grafton Inn, which was built in 1801, and I wondered if the people gathered on the spacious porch noticed how many times I had driven past. With my knowledge from many years of seeking elusive gravestones and hidden burial grounds, I did eventually manage to find what I was looking for. My notes detailed that this one-of-a-kind gravestone was somewhere in the nearby woods. As the day wore on, I decided that it might be best to ask a local, despite the strange look I anticipated getting.

A man was taking down a flag outside of the Grafton Historical Society. When I explained to the friendly gentleman the mission I was on, he proceeded to tell me not only where the grave was but also that he was related to the person whose grave I was seeking. I couldn't believe my luck, and I was thrilled that he invited me into the museum even though they had just closed. Some of the things that caught my eye immediately were the footstones in the glass display case. I asked why they weren't in the local graveyard, and his answer totally surprised me. I was told that sometimes, people would remove the footstones from burial sites, bring them home, warm them up next to the fireplace and use them as bed warmers. I gathered up my purchase of books, videos and pamphlets, along with my newly acquired directions to the grave. In my hand was a pamphlet written by the historical society called *Releasing Rebecca*.

I drove down a dirt road that went into the forest, and it came to an end at the Burgess Cemetery. At the edge of the small dirt parking area are rusty brown, velvet-top mushrooms. The elaborate cemetery gates were quite a surprise to see. There are two marble gravestones side by side that have sleeping lambs carved on top of them. The carving on one stone reads, "Little Carrie," and the other reads, "Little Arthur."

A dramatic smoke tree draws visitors toward the left side of the cemetery, where a tilted slate gravestone reads, "Mrs R. Park / 14 / Children." When walking around to view the headstone, the breathtaking carving and inscription were some of the most heartbreaking I had ever seen in a New England graveyard.

> *In Memory of*
> *Thomas K. Park Junr.*
> *And thirteen infants,*
> *Children of Mr. Thomas K. Park and*
> *Rebecca his wife.*
> *Youth shed a teer,*
> *Se fourteen children slumber here,*
> *Se their image, how they shine,*
> *Like flowers of a fruitful vine.*
> *In Memory of Mrs. Rebecca Park Wife of*
> *Mr. Thomas Park*
> *Who died Septr. 23rd, 1803*
> *In the 40th year of her age.*
> *Behold and fear as you pass by,*
> *My fourteen children with me lie,*
> *Old or young you soon must die,*
> *And turn to dust as well as I.*

During Rebecca Park's life, there was no modern medicine and there were no hospitals; most women gave birth at home, surrounded by family and friends. There would have been no prenatal care to prevent complications at birth. There was a high infant and maternal mortality rate, and giving birth carried a number of untold risks.

The double gravestone was carved by master stone-carver Moses Wright Jr. from Rockingham, Vermont. The columns on the borders of the stone are representative of the pillars of a doorway or gate. The round face that is boxed in is symbolic of the body in the coffin. There are stylized willow branches vining and arching across the top of the lunette. In the center of the double stone is another round-faced soul effigy representing Thomas Park Jr., who died in 1804. Thirteen faces in an arch connected by wavy lines to a center trunk represent the tree of life. Rebecca gave birth to fifteen children over her

Above: A closeup of Rebecca Park's gravestone reveals a tree of life with a face for each child lost.

Right: The stones for Rebecca Park and her fourteen children were created by Moses Wright of Rockingham.

forty years of life. Only one child, Hezekiah, survived to adulthood. He lived to the age of fifty-nine and was buried in Magnolia, Illinois.

A closer examination of the bottom of the Park gravestone reveals practice carvings and random letters. One cannot help but stand in awe of not only the moving gravestone art but also the story of Rebecca. She was a woman who, despite devastating circumstances, continued to try to add children to her family. How does one sum up the incredible story of a woman who surely endured so much grief in her life? Seeing the somber collection of faces on this one-of-a-kind gravestone in the woods of Vermont was one of the most unforgettable moments in my travels.

OLD BENNINGTON CEMETERY

Bennington

The Old First Church in Bennington is called Vermont's "Colonial Shrine," a reference to its founding by those who were seeking religious freedom. Next to the church is the Old Bennington Cemetery, sometimes referred to as "Vermont's Sacred Acre." It contains the remains of those who "labored for the stability and prosperity of Vermont." For those who seek to understand the uncertainties and hardships many of the first settlers experienced, all one needs to do is to step beyond the scenic gates of this cemetery. As visitors enter the cemetery through the gate, a small sign gives a brief history of the cemetery:

> *In 1766 the Proprietors, who were both church leaders and the town government, set aside three acres in the center of the town for the meetinghouse, a burying ground and an animal pound. The present church was built between 1805 & 1806 on the burying ground. However, before construction began family members could exhume their relatives in place, and the gravestones were removed and piled outside the church until after the Civil War. William Montaque petitioned the selectmen to allow him to improve the cemetery at his expense. It was agreed upon, and the grave stones were set "upright and regular."*

The Town of Bennington owns the cemetery and the land under the church. In 1907, the State of Vermont chartered the Bennington Centre Cemetery Association to care for and maintain the graves, which it does today.

A tall, white marble cenotaph is on display between the rows of gravestones, telling the story of Captain Samuel Robinson. The stones says that he was "The Pioneer In The Settlement of Bennington." He was born in Cambridge, Massachusetts, and moved with a group of people to a settlement that became known as Hardwick, Massachusetts. There, he became captain of the town's militia. In 1760, as he was leading his company back from Lake George, they took the wrong branch of the Hoosic River and ended up discovering the lands that would later become Bennington. After his return to Hardwick. Captain Robinson went to Portsmouth, New Hampshire, and bought the land in the chartered wilderness town of Bennington. He held church services in his cabin starting in 1762. In 1767, he represented area landowners in a dispute with New York, and he delivered a petition to King George in England. While there, he was stricken with smallpox and died, and he was buried in London, England. The Bennington marker was commissioned by his grandson David Robinson. The grave for David is particularly interesting, as it states that he was "born on the eve of the Bennington battle, August 15th, 1777."

The first person buried in the cemetery was Bridget Harwood, who was a widow when she moved from Massachusetts with some of her children. She was the first settler to die in Bennington. Her grandson Benjamin Harwood was born in 1762, and he was the first child born in the town. There are a number of notable people, military heroes, ministers and pioneers, buried here, and wandering the rows of gravestones is akin to thumbing through Vermont's history books. Dr. Jonas Fay, the author of the Vermont State Constitution, is buried here. There are five Vermont governors, many of whom owned successful business enterprises as well, buried on the grounds as well.

A long brick platform, cut low on one side so that the marble slab that covers it may catch the full light of the setting sun, tells, in part, the story of an English immigrant who left a lasting impact—both figuratively and literally—on the state of Vermont. The platform reads: "Anthony Haswell, a patriot of the Revolution. Printer and Founder of the Vermont Gazette, 1783. A sufferer in the cause of freedom under the Sedition Act of 1798. Died May 22, 1816, aged 60."

Haswell brought with him the Daye press, the oldest printing press in the country at the time, from which he printed the *Gazette*, Vermont's first newspaper. He gave remarks about and support for Congressman Matthew Lyon, who served as a colonel with the Green Mountain Boys and played an important role in the capture of Fort Ticonderoga in 1775. Lyon had written a series of public letters that attacked President John Adams. On October 6, 1798, Lyon was arrested, and the warrant read that he was a "malicious and seditious person, and of a depraved mind and a wicked and diabolical disposition." Lyon was sentenced to pay a $1,000 fine and serve four months in the jail at Vergennes, so Haswell decided to raise money to pay the fine and have him released. Lyon did not want to be released, as being imprisoned furthered his cause and helped his accusations gain more momentum regarding the wrongs he perceived were being practiced by the government. Haswell accused Federal Marshal Jabez Fitch of being a "hard hearted savage" in print. Haswell was found guilty in a Windsor court, and he was sentenced to two months in prison with a fine of $200. While he was in prison, his twelve-year-old daughter, Mary, died, and he wasn't permitted to go to her funeral. Haswell was released from prison on July 9, 1800, and he returned to Bennington. The town had delayed its Fourth of July celebration until his release, and the cannon was sounded to celebrate not only the country's birthday but also the occasion of his release.

In the center of the cemetery is a marker that was dedicated by the Bennington Historical Society in 1896; it reads, "Around this stone lie buried many patriots who fell in the Battle of Bennington August 16th, 1777. Here also rest British soldiers, Hessians, who died from wounds after the battle. As captives, they were confined in the first meetinghouse built in Vermont, which stood on the green west of this burying ground."

Farther into the cemetery is the grave marker of Charles Cresson Jones, the superintendent of Fillmore Farms at the Colgate Estate, which was a four-thousand-acre farm known in part for its English sheep. Charles had traveled to England to find more stock for the farm and to contract an English housekeeper. Unfortunately, Charles purchased a first-class ticket on board the ill-fated *Titanic* for his return trip to America. When the ocean liner struck an iceberg, according to a witness, Charles assisted people into the lifeboats. When the last lifeboat was cast off, he stood back and calmly lit a cigar, perhaps, some speculate, resigning himself to his

Opposite: William Ellery Channing was a theologian, poet and Unitarian minister and his work was influential on the Transcendental movement.

Above: The First Congregational Church of Bennington adjacent to the cemetery was built in 1805.

fate. His body was recovered by the ship *Mackay-Bennet* and returned to Bennington for burial. An article in the *Bennington Banner* speculated that Jones had a premonition of his death before his voyage. The article stated that "for weeks before he left Fillmore he told the boys his 'heart was not in the trip.'" Fillmore's assistant Charlie Brettle was quoted as saying that Jones also said, "I'll never return. My books and accounts are all in good shape, and I want you to take charge of them."

One of the most visited graves in the cemetery can be found down the hill, a short distance along the tree-lined border of the cemetery. Robert Frost was born in San Francisco, California, and his family moved to Boston,

In Memory of the Revᵈ. Mʳ.
JEDIDIAH DEWEY First Pastor of the
Church in Bennington, Who after
a Laborious Life In the Gospel

Opposite: The grave of Robert Frost in Bennington, Vermont.

Left: The replacement gravestone for Jedidiah Dewey is identical to the original stone.

Massachusetts, after the death of his father. He was a farmer, teacher, poet and author who briefly attended Dartmouth College in New Hampshire and eventually spent just under two years at Harvard University. He was the first poet asked to speak at a presidential inauguration, and on January 20, 1961, which was described as a bitterly cold, sunny day, he recited his poem "The Gift Outright" for President John F. Kennedy. Robert Frost was also named the Poet Laureate of Vermont and was honored with four Pulitzer Prizes. During a seven-year period, Frost's wife, daughter and son all died and were all buried in the same family plot. Beneath Frost's name is the inscription "I had a lover's quarrel with the world," which is the last line of a poem he wrote in 1941 called "A Lesson for Today." For many years, visitors to the grave would leave stones, pennies or mementos; however, this is frowned upon, and a sign tells visitors not to leave tributes on the stone.

The old gravestones here have seemingly survived winter snows, frost heaves, wildlife encounters and all the challenges that nature can bring. However, in the spring of 2008, the gravestone for Reverend Jedidiah Dewey was broken completely off its concrete base. An exact replica stone was commissioned in Barre by Charles Dewey, a descendant of the reverend, and was put in place in 2010 at the cemetery. To preserve the original stone, it was donated to the Bennington Museum, where it is on display to help share the history of the community. The original stone was carved and signed by prolific gravestone-carver Frederick Manning. The Mannings were carvers from Connecticut, and their work was detailed with distinctive symbolism of the highest quality. There is the stylized soul effigy carved on the stone, complete with clerical tabs that would have been worn by the reverend. A symbol of transformation, a butterfly is found at the center of the stone, and on each side, a dove symbolizes the ascension of the soul or spirit to heaven. Trees are found along the stone's border, and a heart in the center represents that the soul continues on and is made victorious over death.

The Reverend Jedediah Dewey came to Bennington from Westfield, Massachusetts, and was the first minister in Bennington. He served until his death in 1778. Part of the inscription on his stone reads:

> *Of comfort no man speak!*
> *Let's talk of graves, and worms, and epitaphs;*
> *Make dust our paper, and with rainy eyes*
> *Write sorrow on the bosom of the earth.*

It is important to note that there are a variety of important gravestone carvers represented in the cemetery, including Zerrubbael Collins, Samuel Dwight, Roger Booth and Ebenezer Soule. There are several signs throughout the grounds indicating which stones are attributed to certain carvers. An unusual marble stone with four arches (lunettes) carved by Roger Booth marks the grave of sixteen-year-old Lucy Hatheway, who died in 1794, and the three infants of Mr. Levy and Mrs. Esther Hatheway. An intricately carved woman in a mourning dress next to a funerary urn is depicted on the stone of Honorable David Fay, who died in 1827. He was a Vermont Supreme Court judge and United States attorney under President Thomas Jefferson.

Dellwood Cemetery

Manchester

The town of Manchester, Vermont, has always been situated at the perfect crossroads for travelers. A cultural center with a treasure trove of iconic

One of the many angel monuments found at the Dellwood Cemetery in Manchester, Vermont.

architecture, it remains a vibrant village for visitors with an abundance of outdoor activities. Settled in 1764, the community grew quickly, and its original burial ground was no longer adequate by the mid-nineteenth century. *The History of Bennington County* tells us:

> *When the old churchyard in the village became filled with graves, a beautiful spot was selected at the south end of the village for a new graveyard, and this too in time became overcrowded. The Hon. Mark Skinner of Chicago, and Hon. Helmus Wells of New York, former residents of the village, seeing the necessity of enlarging the grounds, purchased adjoining land and presented it to an association that would improve and ornament it. In 1865 Dellwood Cemetery Association was incorporated, by an act of the Legislature, and the land, about thirteen acres, was conveyed to the association by Messrs, Skinner and Wells.*

About six thousand dollars was subscribed for the embellishment of the grounds, and the work was accomplished under the supervision of Burton A. Thomas, a skillful rural architect.

The avenues and walks wind about artistically over the ore elevated ground and into the valleys beneath, and along the beautiful creek, by the damming of which a pond is formed at either end of the cemetery, and along the course are one or more waterfalls. The stream is spanned by several rustic bridges. Under the bluff, with a broad carriage way in front, is situated the receiving vault, surmounted by bronze griffins. Hedges of cedar, hemlock, and arbor vitae in various parts of the grounds add beauty and picturesqueness to the view. In summer the margins of the walks are lined with beautiful flowers and foliage plants from the greenhouse of the association. Many handsome monuments and vases adorn the grounds. The highly ornamental gateway at the main entrance was the gift of Judge Skinner. Just outside the gate, on the left stands a marble pedestal surmounted by a statue of "Mourning" depositing flowers. On the right, on a similar pedestal, a statue of "Gabriel" with trumpet in hand, personifies the "Resurrection." On the large gate-posts are ornamental bronze vases, from which in summer time flowers and vines grow in harmonious profusion. In keeping with the other appointments at Dellwood is the beautiful residence occupied by the superintendent. This is a substantial stone structure standing near the north end of the grounds. It is occupied by Mr. George Smith, under whose care and attention the cemetery increases in beauty with each succeeding year.

Within the confines of the Dellwood Cemetery is the grave of John S. Pettibone, who died in 1872. He was a probate judge who represented Vermont in the General Assembly from 1822 to 1842, and a curious document written by him regarding vampirism can be found in the archives of the Manchester Historical Society. Rachel Harris, who was described as a beautiful young woman, married Captain Isaac Burton, a deacon in the Congregational church in 1789. Although Rachel was in good health when she married, less than one year after her wedding day, she became deathly ill and succumbed to consumption at the age of twenty-one. Captain Burton married a woman named Hulda Powell almost two years after the death of Rachel. Hulda was also in good health at the time of her marriage; however, within months of the marriage, she became ill as well. She displayed the same symptoms as Rachel: coughing up blood with an ashen face and extended lethargy. The notion came to some of the family and friends that perhaps a vampire had killed Rachel and was now going after Hulda. Some people even suspected that Rachel may have been a vampire; they said she had come back for revenge on Captain Burton's new wife.

Judge John S. Pettibone wrote the following published account:

> *They were induced to believe that if the vitals of the first wife could be consumed by being burned in a charcoal fire, it would affect a cure of the sick second wife. Such was a strange delusion that they disinterred the first wife who had been buried about three years. They took out the liver, heart, and lungs, what remained of them, and burned them to ashes on the blacksmith forge of Jacob Mead. Timothy Mead officiated at the altar in the sacrifice to the Demon Vampire who it was believed, was still sucking the blood of the then living wife of Captain Burton. It was the month of February and good sleighing. Such was the excitement that from five hundred to one thousand people were present. The account was furnished me by an eye witness of the transaction.*

Despite the actions taken with the body of Rachel, Hulda died on September 6, 1793. Isaac Burton's grave can be found at the Dellwood Cemetery in Manchester, where he was buried with his fourth wife, Dency. Rachel's gravestone stands in the Factory Point Cemetery on Cemetery Avenue in Manchester.

A small marble gravestone in Dellwood reads, "Miss Icy Palmer, Born Sept. 1824, Died July 9, 1911. Asleep in Jesus." Icy was a local legend in Manchester, and a recollection of her in the *Manchester Journal* from January 27, 1955, describes her as "Black-shawled Icy, with frayed umbrella in hand, always stopping to look behind her!" Icy was a Tuscarora Native from the Carolinas who was allegedly brought to town by a Native tribe and given away when she was only a few weeks old, as her family was continuing their voyage north in the winter. One version of her origin story states that she was abandoned in a sugar house in town. She was originally named Louisa, but she later changed her name. She was taken in by two families: the G.S. Purdys and W.P. Blacks. The Ladies Benevolent Society provided her with a home on River Road; however, she continued to wander around town in all forms of weather. In her travels, she found opportunities to assist local families in need. With her independent nature and odd ways, she was said to be "mysterious" by some.

She loved to learn, and she would collect natural items and create enchanted ritual candles that she would burn for protection from dusk until dawn. She also sold these candles to tourists. She was also a fortune

The wingspan of this carved angel at Dellwood Cemetery is about ten feet wide.

teller at the nearby Equinox Hotel, and President Lincoln's eldest son, Robert Todd Lincoln, sought her out for her advice and prophecies. She lived independently until about the age of eighty, when it was determined by the locals that she needed care, as her mind was beginning to fail. She was escorted to the Brattleboro Retreat, the first facility for the care of the mentally ill in Vermont, in 1909. Icy said she found it "sumptuous." She died peacefully in her sleep, and her obituary called her a landmark of the town. A funeral service was held for her in a chamber of the local church, but because she was Native, she was not given a proper ceremony. Known by most people in town, she was never treated as an equal due to her heritage, yet she purchased her burial plot beside them at Dellwood.

Some of the other wonderful features of the Dellwood Cemetery are the many life-sized statues of angels. One of the most magnificent can be seen at the grave of Arthur Taylor, who died by suicide with a single gunshot wound to the head at the age of forty in New York City in 1905. This incredible marble angel features expansive feathery wings, a folded dress, a delicate necklace and a bare foot stepping onto a pillow. Oftentimes, tiny treasures can be found resting in its folded hands, like feathers, beach stones and beaded jewelry left from visitors.

There is also a receiving tomb that was used for winter storage at the edge of the cemetery. When Robert Todd Lincoln died, his body was stored here while arrangements were made to transfer his remains to Arlington National Cemetery in Virginia. He died in his sleep at his summer home in Manchester, the Hildene, from a cerebral hemorrhage at the age of eighty-two in 1926.

SAINT JAMES CEMETERY

Arlington, Vermont

The Saint James Episcopal Church Cemetery exhibits the care and consideration, along with the restoration, that every graveyard of this age should see. There are over five hundred graves here, and the first interment occurred in 1777. A two-story wooden church known as the Bethel Church originally stood on the site; however, it burned down, and the current church was built in 1831. The rows of gravestones here are neatly arranged and easy to navigate. The condition of the stones is quite remarkable, as most of them are easy to read, offering up the tiniest of artistic details. Underfoot is a carpet of the fragrant and spicy-scented herb thyme. Thyme was often planted in graveyards to mask the scent of decay, and sprigs would have been put in coffins as well.

The striking nature of the gravestones displaying a variety of facial expressions and dispositions, some with their tiny hands holding hearts,

The condition of the gravestones at the Saint James Episcopal Church Cemetery are in remarkable condition.

vines and flowers, is an absolute delight to view. The gravestone for ten-year-old Miriam Hawley, who died in 1796, depicts a fanciful wave of long hair curled around a sweetly smiling face. On Miriam's footstone is a single daisy surrounded by flourishes. An angel with their hands over their heart and a halo that reads "Memento Mori" (Remember Death) is on the gravestone

The gravestone for young Adoniram Hawley, who died in 1792, depicts a figure with closed eyes.

of John Canfield, who died at the age of ten years and nine months in 1796.

Many of the stones here are signed at the very bottom by Zerubabbel Collins of Shaftsbury, Vermont. It has been speculated that he would make an effort at times to show the age of the deceased through his carvings, offering sunken cheekbones or other distinctive features. Gravestone-carver Samuel Dwight is also represented here. Henry Rule was a gravestone-carver who had come to the area from Scotland; he has a few stones here and he was buried on the grounds with his wife, Mary Canfield.

The inscription on the grave of Jedediah Aylesworth reads:

Son of Abel & Freelove Aylesworth
This youth though was lov'd by all
By old and young by great and small
Hid generous soul his obliging way
Amongst his acquaintances bore their sway
But death that conqueror bowed his head
And now he lies among the dead
Yet he shall rise and leave the ground
When the archangel gives the sound

He was sixteen years, six months and nine days old when he died in March 1795 from smallpox, which he had contracted while taking a load of provisions to his sister in Cayuga County, New York.

There are several founders of the church who are buried here, as well as many soldiers who were part of the Green Mountain Boys. Mary Brownson Allen, the wife of Ethan Allen, was buried here along with their two children, Joseph and Mary. A marker erected for her by the Daughters of the American Revolution in 1895 can be found here. A variety of ornate Victorian gravestones can be found toward the back of the graveyard; some of these stones measure four to five feet tall. It is quite easy to lose track of time wandering this historic cemetery, as there is so much to see and discover here.

Left: The gravestone for Mary Lyon has a smiling carved angel with tiny arms outstretched. Mary died at the age of thirty-nine in 1784.

Below: Four spires rise up from the back of the Saint James Episcopal Church Cemetery in Arlington, Vermont.

DUMMERSTON VERMONT

The town of Dummerston, Vermont, contains a few burial places that have been lost to time over the years. The town records report what happened to the earliest graveyard.

> *The first burials in the town were made in the old grave-yard, formerly in Dummerston, now in Putney, about 40 rods northwest from the railroad station. In 1873, seventeen old gravestones were left standing in the yard, and at the present time only nine remain. The rest have been broken down and trampled in pieces by cattle. The grave of Capt. John Kathan, the first settler in Dummerston, is, therefore, left unmarked. Quite a number of the first settlers must have been buried in that yard; for in making the excavation for a cellar on its site a few years ago, seven bodies or skeletons were found, and the owner of the land states that his horses sometimes step into soft places where graves were dug.*

Located on East-West Road is the Dummerston Center Cemetery. The expansive grounds yield views of the nearby farm fields and surrounding hills in the distance. Near the center of the cemetery are six dark and weathered gravestones for members of the Spaulding family. Lieutenant Leonard Spaulding was from Westford, Massachusetts and he was a war hero having served in the French and Indian War as well as the American Revolution. He spent the final years of his life in Dummerston with his wife and eleven children. A grim shadow fell over the Spaulding household in the 1780s. The agony of consumption had claimed seven of the Spaulding children in 1788. It wasn't long before fearful family members believed that it was a cursed vine that wrapped around the family's coffins. The belief was that another person would die as the vine evolved. In order to survive the curse, the last Spaulding who died was disinterred for an unsettling curse-breaking ritual.

Regarding the record of the incident, it is recorded in the *Vermont Historical Gazetteer* in 1891:

> *It is related by those who remember the circumstances; after six or seven of the family had died of consumption, another daughter was taken, it was supposed, with the same disease. It was thought she would die, and much was said in regard to so many of the family's dying of consumption when they all seemed to have the appearance of good health and long life. Among the superstitions of those days, we find it was said that a vine or root of*

Was there a poisonous vine that caused vampirism going through the grave of Mary Spaulding in Dummerston, Vermont?

some kind grew from coffin to coffin, of those of one family, who died of consumption, and were buried side by side; and when the growing vine had reached the coffin of the last one buried, another one of the family would die; the only way to destroy the influence or effect, was to break the vine; take up the body of the last one buried and burn the vitals; which would be an effectual remedy: Accordingly, the body of the last one, buried was dug up and the vitals taken out and burned, and the daughter, it is affirmed, got well and lived many years. The act, doubtless, raised her mind from a state of despondency to hopefulness.

The exhumation of the body and the burning of the vital organs was an acceptable cure to break the effects of the cursed vine. Could it have been true, or was it all just a coincidence?

3

SOUTH-CENTRAL VERMONT

THE GRAVE OF JOSEPH WAIT

Clarendon

The scenic town of Clarendon, Vermont, is home to several cemeteries, but there is one lonesome gravestone in the middle of a cornfield, surrounded by a chain-link fence. The white marble gravestone is particularly eye-catching, with a relief carving of a man in a Revolutionary uniform and hat with a sword held high. Joseph Wait was born in November 1732 in Sudbury, Massachusetts. His military career was a combination of spectacular adventures and important historical events. By 1755, Joseph had been appointed corporal and was part of a regiment assigned in western Massachusetts, which was part of a campaign to subdue French forces during the Seven Years' War. The conflict was between France and Great Britain and began as a dispute over North American land claims in 1754. Joseph was part of a 180-man expedition sent to Fort Ticonderoga to learn about troop strategies west of the fort in 1758. The men in the expedition traveled on ice skates and snowshoes.

The rangers were overcome, and only fifty-five soldiers managed to escape to the northern edge of Lake George. Challenging conditions continued as the group planned their way through the wilderness headed toward the Connecticut River. Joseph and his brother Benjamin were side by side in that treacherous retreat. It was reported that supplies had become so low that the soldiers had to eat beechnuts, and they boiled leather for nourishment.

One popular story about Joseph described that he shot a deer—and not a moment too soon, as his men were suffering from extreme hunger. After feeding his company, he carved his initials into a tree and hung the deer meat there for the next division of rangers to find. The next group of soldiers did find the food, and they, too, were able to carry on. A nearby river that flows into the Connecticut River was named Waits River to commemorate this hopeful turn of events.

In the following years, there were several similar incidents, as territories, grants and charters continued to be debated and fought for. Sheriff Daniel Whipple from Cumberland County, New York, arrested the Wait brothers for rioting in connection with their sympathies toward the New Hampshire grants. Forty men from Windsor showed up, armed with swords, pistols and clubs, to free the captive brothers. Eventually, Joseph joined Ethan Allen's Green Mountain Boys and served in the capture of Fort Ticonderoga by colonial troops in May 1775. In 1776, Joseph was stationed at Rangers Island in Isle la Motte in Lake Champlain as part of an advanced guard for Benedict Arnold's fleet. He was at the post for about two months before he was struck in the head by a fragment from an exploding gun carriage during a skirmish. On his journey back home through Clarendon, he died on September 28, 1776, at the age of forty-three. His gravestone reads: "In memory of Lt. Col. Joseph Wait, officer in the American Revolutionary War, who died on his return from an expedition into Canada, September 1776. This stone is erected in testimony of respect by his brethren in arms."

ROMAINE TENNEY MEMORIAL

Weathersfield

It was said that early one summer, trouble visited Romaine Tenney. He may have been the only man to fight back an army of bulldozers with a pitchfork. The story goes back to 1892, when Romaine's parents, Myron and Rosa, purchased the ninety-acre Ascutney farm. They had nine children, and as time went on, it was Romaine who remained on the farm as a bachelor with four dogs, three cats, two horses and sixty cows. He had served in the army for two years, starting in 1942. The way he farmed was not unlike the way

The memorial site for Romaine Tenney has a pavilion, informational sign, benches and the stump of the tree that used to be part of his farm.

his parents farmed: without machinery. He did everything by hand or with horses. He lived without electricity in his house and only had it in the barn. When he needed to get around, he often chose to walk or get a ride from someone rather than drive a vehicle. More than just a humble farmer, he was a stubborn Yankee.

When the State Highway Department set its sights on his property in 1964, with the intent to put an interstate highway lane right where his house and farm stood, battle lines were drawn. A judge and jury decided the farm was worth $13,600, which Romaine wasn't the least interested in. He was quoted as saying that he would rather die on the farm than leave. The state moved forward with the process of eminent domain; bulldozers soon arrived on the farm, as no agreement could be reached.

In the dark of night, at 2:00 a.m. on September 12, 1964, a fire blazed through the old Tenney house and two nearby barns. A collection of old sleighs and wagons, which had been removed from the barn under court order, were also on fire. Once the fire was out, there was no immediate sign of Romaine Tenney. However, after closer inspection, it appeared that the fire had been set in four different parts of the house. Fragments of bones and a dental plate were found in the cellar hole. In the end, it was believed that Romaine had lit the fires and gone inside the house to wait for death. The brick Victorian Gothic house, with its diamond-paned windows and gingerbread trim, was gone forever. The highway progressed, and the road was built over the old farm property. For a number of years, some neighbors who believed Romaine might still be alive left plates of food in the nearby woods.

A large maple tree remained on the property after the fire and became a memorial of sorts to Romaine Tenney. However, in 2021, it was determined that the massive tree was rotting from the inside out and needed to be cut down. The memories of Romaine and his plight are still very much alive with local residents. A decision was made to build a pavilion to honor Romaine and the story of his life. The Agency of Transportation put forth a $30,000 grant to pay for its construction. The tree was cut down, and today, the stump remains with a small circle of flowers around it. A large informational marker with photographs can now be found on the site. Several local people showed an interest in collecting the wood from the tree in memory of Romaine Tenney. One man from Brattleboro used the wood to construct a violin and violas. The Tenney family still owns approximately twenty acres on the other side of Route 91. According to Tenney's descendants, they still tell the story about how Romaine lived and died. The memorial can be visited just off exit 8, next to the parking area on Route 91.

Marble Town

Proctor

The history and industry of Proctor, Vermont, is proudly on display and immediately visible once you cross the town line. The brilliant and striking white marble arch bridge that crosses over Otter Creek was built in 1915. The bridge was given to the town by Emily Dutton Proctor as a memorial to her son Fletcher D. Proctor. The town was named for the Honorable Redfield Proctor, who was raised near Cavendish, Vermont. His mother, Betsy, raised him alone from the time he was eight years old, after his father died suddenly. He graduated Albany Law School and practiced in Boston, Massachusetts. He worked his way up in the military and eventually was the commander of the Fifteenth Vermont Regiment and the Gettysburg

Campaign. He became the governor of Vermont in 1878, and his two sons, Fletcher and Redfield, also both became governors of Vermont. He was appointed the receiver of the Sutherland Falls Company, a growing marble company that helped the town become known as the marble capital of Vermont. By 1880, the Sutherland Falls Marble Company had become the Vermont Marble Company. Within five years, the volume of marble the company produced had grown so swiftly that not only gravestones were being produced, but other building materials were being made as well. The United States Supreme Court building and the Jefferson Memorial were constructed out of marble from the company's quarries. By 1886, the name of the settlement, which was originally Sutherland Falls, was changed to Proctor.

The Sutherland Waterfalls generated the waterpower for the mills and shops in Proctor that sawed and finished the marble. The waterfall is 122 feet tall and flows into Otter Creek, generating over three thousand horsepower. It was said that people immigrated from as many as thirty-six different nations around the world to Proctor during its heyday. The company encouraged its employees to build their own houses, and many of these fine houses still exist with shining Proctor marble foundations. The sidewalks around town were also constructed using white marble, as was the hospital and the fire department. Even swampy parts of the town were filled in with pieces of marble.

Redfield Proctor went on to become the secretary of war from 1889 to 1891. He died on March 4, 1908, and the newspaper reports from every corner of the state contained words of honor and praise for his public service. The *Rutland News* printed the following:

> *The monarch oak, the patriarch of trees, shoots rising up. Supreme in state. The oak has been felled, but only by the omnipotent axman—ripe in years. Sturdy and strong he stood for fifty years of magnificent mental, moral, and physical stature, the sentinel of the state and the exemplar of New England character as typified in Vermont. Buffeted by the elements, hacked at by petty inimical creatures of the woods, he withstood all, ruggedly, majestically, unmarred, because his fiber was true and sound.*

Redfield Proctor was interred with his wife, Emily, their children and other family members in the Proctor mausoleum at the South Street Cemetery. The mausoleum was built using Proctor marble and has Ionic columns in the neoclassical style. Fittingly, the grounds of the cemetery were

HONORING
THE HERITAGE OF
VERMONT MARBLE WORKERS

Theophile Juaire Canada	John Peter Lind Sweden
John Lebo, Sr. Austria-Hungary	Otto V. Gustafson Sweden
Rodolf H. Hollmann Germany	Oscar A. Gustafson Sweden
John Baro Poland	John Alfred Johnson Sweden
Fritz Gollstrom Sweden	John Edwin Jacobson Sweden
Axel Anderson Norway	Andrew Macek Czechoslovakia
Antonio Manganelli Italy	Arvid E. Johnson Sweden
Axel Sarcka Finland	Louis A. King Canada
Waldemar Siriane Finland	Swan Olaf Mattsson Sweden
Carl S. Hedon Sweden	Antoni Tatarinowicz Belarus
Oscar L. Johnson Sweden	Boleslaw Tatarinowicz Belarus
John Galles, Sr.	Stanislaw Tatarinowicz Belarus
Ivan Jilinski Czechoslovakia	Ivar Hella Finland
Louis Skottet Norway	Swan Swanson Sweden
	Oskar Hella Finland

Opposite, top: Looking across from the South Street Cemetery, you can view the beautiful, white marble church Saint Dominics.

Opposite, bottom: The remains of the founder of the town and his family can be found in the Proctor Mausoleum.

Above: One of the marble worker's memorial stones at the Vermont Marble Museum in Proctor.

given to the town by Redfield himself in 1889. In the nineteenth century, the inhabitants of Proctor were described as harmonious, and it was said that the Protestant and Catholic cemeteries were joined without any fence or separation between the two, a marble wall running across the front of each. From the cemetery hillside, the marble town seems to glow around the view of Saint Dominic's Roman Catholic Church, which was built in 1925 in the New England Gothic Revival style using Ashland marble. On Ormsby Avenue is the grave of old Charlie Redfield, Redfield Proctor's Civil War Morgan horse. A twenty-ton block of marble with a sundial marks the grave. Just down the road is the Vermont Marble Museum on Main Street. In front of the museum is a large slab of marble honoring the heritage of Vermont marble workers. Many of the workers remembered on the stone are buried in the South Cemetery.

CONGREGATIONAL CEMETERY

Castleton

Bird Mountain is one of the northernmost peaks in the Taconic Range, which was formed approximately 440 million years ago. The mountain rises 2,500 feet above sea level and is composed of rocky quartz. There are sharp and steep precipices on the mountain, making it quite challenging to climb. The mountain is named for Colonel Amos Bird, who traveled with two other men from Salisbury, Connecticut. He was eventually separated from the group in what is now the town of Castleton, Vermont. Unable to find his companions, he fell asleep on top of the mountain. When he opened his eyes in the morning, he discovered that he had fallen asleep on a very steep ledge. From that vantage point, Colonel Bird stood up and got a bird's eye view of the area.

After exploring the area and joining back up with his party, Bird went back to Connecticut, only to return four years later with several other families to make a permanent settlement. He even found the perfect spot for a sawmill in what is now known as Hydeville. Colonel Byrd became quite ill immediately after the sawmill was built, and the first work done by his mill was sawing the boards for his coffin. He was buried on the banks of the Castleton River, two miles west of the village, by his request. In 1842, his body was moved to the old cemetery in Castleton, and a monument made of Rutland marble and an obelisk were placed on his grave. The monument reads:

> *Colonel Amos, Byrd, erected by the citizens of Castleton and friends, as a tribute of respect to a worthy man, born in Salisbury, Connecticut, and died September 16, 1770 to age 30 years. Colonel Amos Byrd was the first white man who asserted dominion in Castleton, where he arrived in June 1766. He was the first possessor of the soil for civilization and the first called to resign it, leaving the fruits of his bold enterprise to others.*
>
> *The mortal remains of Colonel Bird were first interred at his direction near his dwelling in the valley of Birds creek two miles west of this place, and after 70 years disinterred here reinterred to wade the summons that awakes the dead.*

In 1886, the Lee lodge of Freemasons chose Bird Mountain as the location of their summer picnic. Not only did the Masons of Castleton gather, but they were also joined by others from surrounding towns on August 27, 1886, to climb the mountain with a special purpose. Each participant carried a brick two by eight inches long and bore their name and the name of their lodge. The monument contained 756 stone blocks, and it was said that two thousand people visited the mountain that day. Looking at the mountain from a distance, the enormous monument was visible from the village. However, during a severe thunderstorm on September 18, 1898, the monument was struck by lightning, leaving it in ruins. Sometime afterward, the Masons climbed the mountain to retrieve the remaining stones, which were then used to build the fireplace in the Masonic temple in Castleton. All that remains of the monument is a rough weathered stone that used to be its base.

JAMES HARTNESS, SUMMERHILL CEMETERY

Springfield

James Hartness was a renaissance man in the world of mechanical engineering, but that is only one part of the genius of a man who was not only an inventor but also the governor of Vermont. He was born in New

York in 1861. He eventually found his way to Springfield, Vermont, where he became the company president of Jones and Lamson Machine Company. He was the holder of over 120 patents, including those for several types of machinery components. He built his mansion in Springfield in 1904, which encompassed all of 35 acres.

The worlds of flight, aerospace and astronomy all intrigued James, and he was deeply involved in each. He built his own telescope in 1910, and it was state of the art at the time. It was the first ever rotating telescope in the world, calibrated to view each planet in our solar system. The telescope was housed in a futuristic observatory connected to a massive tunnel system beneath his house. The 250-foot-long tunnel was connected to eight underground rooms, a workshop and even a bar. The rooms had water pipes and electricity and a door that led out to the street. He was one of the first one hundred licensed pilots in the country, and in 1919, he built the first airport in Vermont. After Charles Lindbergh made his transatlantic flight, he stayed at the Hartness Estate in Springfield.

During his two-year term as governor, Hartness was concerned that too many people from Vermont were leaving the state to live elsewhere. He

What secrets lie beneath the lawn of the Hartness House in Springfield, Vermont?

The graves of inventors James and Lena Hartness in Springfield, Vermont.

felt that the solution to this was to build a strong transportation industry. When he passed away on February 2, 1934, at the age of seventy-two, the newspapers reported that, even though he achieved greatness, he never lost the "common touch." The day of his funeral, all places of business and schools in Springfield were closed out of respect for his memory, and an airplane circled slowly over the town in a tribute to the man who brought the development of aviation to Vermont.

He was buried at Summerhill Cemetery in Springfield, just a five-minute walk from his home. James rests next to his wife, Lena, who was an inventor as well. Their house still stands, and the tunnels remain under the front lawn. Listed in the National Register of Historic Places, the property is now a well-appointed hotel. Many visitors have claimed that the hotel is haunted by James, and items have even been known to move off the walls in the tunnel rooms. The hotel's website speaks of James's eccentricities and the occasional ghostly sighting.

VAMPIRES IN SOUTH WOODSTOCK, VERMONT

A shocking incident involving vampirism in South Woodstock, Vermont, took place in 1817, according to the Woodstock History Center. The story concerned a young man by the name of Frederick Ransom, who was buried in the Ransom-Kendall Cemetery in South Woodstock. Frederick's brother Daniel Ransom wrote the following in 1894 about Frederick and the burning of his heart:

> *Frederick Ransom, the second son of my father and mother, was born in South Woodstock, Vermont, June 16, 1797 and died of consumption February 14, 1817 at the age of about twenty. He had a good education and was a member of Dartmouth college at the time of his death. My remembrance of him is quite limited as I was only three years at the time of his death....It has been related to me that there was a tendency in our family to consumption....It seems that Father shared somewhere in the idea of hereditary diseases, and withal had some superstition, for it was said that if the heart of one of the family who died of consumption was taken out and burned, others would be free from it. And Father, having some faith in the remedy, had the heart of Frederick taken out after he had been buried, and it was burned in Captain Pearson's blacksmith forge. However, it did not prove a remedy, for mother, sister, and two brothers died of that disease afterward.*

Daniel's brother Royal Ransom was an assistant justice of the Windsor County Court who died from consumption at the age of thirty-three in 1832. The family can be found buried in the Ransom-Kendall Cemetery at the top of a hill beyond grazing pastures off Route 106 in South Woodstock.

4

CENTRAL VERMONT

Middlebury Cemetery

Middlebury

One might not expect to find a grave on a college golf course, but a lone marble stone stands with a blue sign to indicate the burial site of William Douglas. He was one of the first settlers of Middlebury, Vermont, and his house stood in the location of the Ralph Myhre Golf Course at Middlebury College. He answered the call of an alarm in Castleton, and he was the ensign under the command of Lieutenant Robert Armstrong in Captain John Stillwell's Company. The rally of the First Vermont Brigade required William to march forty miles to serve in the effort to take lands that were part of New York back for Vermont. His gravestone tells the story of what happened after he returned to Middlebury one day and went into the forest to cut wood.

> *Mr. William Douglas,*
> *Born June 22, 1735, was killed*
> *Instantly by the fall of a tree*
> *Dec. 19, 1783*
> *Here life & all its pleasures end,*
> *Here mourners wander, read & weep;*
> *Soon each succeeds his fallen friend,*
> *And in the same cold bed must sleep.*

Left: The fascinating gravestone of Edward Turner, a professor at Middlebury College.

Right: The gravestone of two-year-old Amun Her Khepeshef, who died in 1883.

On South Main Street is the Middlebury Cemetery (also known as the West Cemetery), and the oldest gravestones here date to the turn of the nineteenth century. One of the first notable gravestones visitors will encounter along the road into the cemetery is the stone of Edward Turner, who was a professor at Middlebury College. The gravestone has a sculptural carving of an all-seeing eye, an hourglass and skull with a dramatic depiction of a snake eating its tail. This symbol, also known as an ouroboros, represents the never-ending cycle of life. The gravestone inscription also reads, "He was a scholar, a husband, father and a Christian." He was forty-one when he died in 1838. A closer inspection of the gravestone reveals that Henry, aged fourteen and a half months, sleeps by his father's side.

Walking into the cemetery, past a few more rows, visitors will run across one of the most unusual residents of Vermont's burial grounds. A gravestone for Amun Her Khepeshef can be found with a cross and two Egyptian symbols: a bird and an ankh, which are supposed to represent the afterlife. A local antiques trader, Henry Sheldon, bought an Egyptian mummy from a New York antique dealer, and he set up the mummy along with other curiosities in his house turned museum. When Henry died, the decaying mummy was

Left: Honey made at Champlain Valley Apiaries, established by Charles Mraz, can be found in specialty stores in Vermont.

Right: A beehive is carved on the gravestone of beekeeper and scientist Charles Mraz.

put into the care of museum trustee George W. Mead, who decided it was best to have the remains cremated and interred at the burial ground. Amun was believed to have been a child of a royal Egyptian family, and his date of death is inscribed on the stone as "1883 B.C."

Toward the middle of the cemetery, a carved beehive can be found on the gravestone of Charles Mraz, who died at the age of ninety-four in 1999. Charles was a world-renowned beekeeper and pioneer of bee sting therapy. In 1928, he moved from New York to Middlebury and established the Champlain Valley Apiaries, which was New England's largest bee apiary. He was a columnist and regular contributor to a variety of publications, and in 1994, he authored a book called *Health and the Honeybee* about his experiences with bee venom therapy. Charles was also a founding member of the American Apitherapy Society, a nonprofit organization that was dedicated to the medical use of bee products. Some of his contributions to commercial beekeeping were tried and true techniques that more efficiently produce and harvest honey. In addition to his many accomplishments and innovations, he was very involved with community affairs and even served on the Middlebury Cemetery Committee.

BEN AND JERRY'S FLAVOR GRAVEYARD

Waterbury, Vermont

A purple archway leads to a truly unique graveyard in Waterbury, Vermont. Thirty-five granite gravestones are lined up in rows, each with a delicious story to tell. Perhaps this is the only graveyard in the state that elicits laughter. Flavor wizards Ben Cohen and Jerry Greenfield have been creating pint-sized pleasures since 1978, when they first sold their ice cream from a scoop shop in Burlington, Vermont. In 1985, Ben and Jerry opened their first factory in Waterbury, which still produces more than 350,000 pints of ice cream each day. The factory quickly became a tourist destination, with people visiting from all over the world, drawn by the amazing power of ice cream. The tours end with samples in the whimsically designed tasting room.

Just up the hill from the bustling factory is the Flavor Graveyard, which is a tribute to the flavors that are no longer bites on the spoon because they've "bitten the dust." It is here that fans grieving the loss of their favorite flavors can find peace—and humor—among the gravestone epitaphs for the dearly de-pinted. Some of the inscriptions you can find in the graveyard read as follows:

Honey I'm Home
Honey Vanilla Ice Cream & Fudge Covered Honeycomb Candy Nuggets
It was a honey of a flavor, But all too brief a love affair, Honey ran away
from home, To new digs you-know-where 2002–2002

Oh Pear
Fresh Pear Ice Cream with a Hint of Almond and a Light Fudge Swirl
Oh Pear, Oh Pear
A mixture of mirth
All nannies did weep When you left of this earth 1997–1997

Holy Cannoli
Creamy Ricotta and Pistachio Ice Cream With Chocolate Covered Cannolis
and Roasted Pistachios
Now in front of the pearly gates,
Holy Cannoli sits and waits.
What brought it to ruin no one knows, Must have been the pistachios.
1997–1998

The gates to the Ben and Jerry's Flavor Graveyard.

Some of the humorous gravestones at the Ben and Jerry's Flavor Graveyard in Waterbury, Vermont.

Also memorialized here in hopes of "rein-conation" are past flavors, like Ethan Almond, Vermonty Python and Wavy Gravy. The sweet folks at the factory will tell you that the graveyard sees about 250,000 visitors every year. The company even takes submissions to "resurrect" flavors from the great beyond on their website. Should you visit this mysterious place, be sure to lower your spoon for a moment of silence as you go through the stages of grief for the flavors that have melted into tasty oblivion.

CUTLER CEMETERY

East Montpelier, Vermont

A palm leaf symbolizing peace and eternal life is carved on the gravestone of Carrie Anna "Annie" Wheeler at the Cutler Cemetery in East Montpelier, Vermont. Annie Wheeler was seventeen when she was murdered on May 29, 1897. Annie was described in the local newspaper as "a pretty, winning maiden." She met Jack Wheeler, "a popular and gentlemanly young man of spotless character" who was a stonecutter by trade. The future seemed promising for the two of them, except for one thing—or rather, one person—Mildred Brewster.

Mildred was described as a "willful girl" whose parents "never had much control over." She had attended school in Burlington for a short time, but she ended up working in a tailor shop in Montpelier. She and Jack had boarded at the same place, and her feelings for him were quite intense. It was uncertain if, in fact, Jack reciprocated the feelings Mildred had for him. However, when Jack met Annie, he was quite taken by her.

Mildred's affections only grew toward him, and she became determined to be with him. According to reports, she "made the wicked resolve to end her unhappy life and also Jack Wheelers." One dark night, Mildred moved forward with a desperate plan in the shadows of the local armory, where Jack was drilling. The local newspaper recounted how the terrifying events unfolded as presented at the following court trial.

> *With revolver in hand she waited to revenge herself because her love was not reciprocated, and had not Jack happened to leave the armory in company with his brother, a tragedy would probably had been enacted that night. But seeing Jack's brother, Mildred gave up the idea of murder for that night.*

A palm leaf is carved on the small stone of Annie Wheeler at Cutler Cemetery in East Montpelier.

When she awoke the next morning the resolve was still firm. Soon after rising she left the house and proceeded up Clay Hill.

Here, near an old building, she practiced shooting at a target for a while and then started to see Miss Annie Wheeler. There was some exchange of words in regard to Jack, both girls asserting that they were engaged to him. Mildred knew that Jack and Miss Wheeler contemplated celebrating Memorial Day at Barre, but made up her mind that they should never go to that city. The two girls decided that they would go and see Jack and talk over the matter of their differences with him. It was a rainy morning and the two girls walked under the same umbrella.

When they were within a few rods of the house where Jack lived, Mildred suddenly turned and drew a revolver, pointing it toward Miss Wheeler and pulled the trigger. A deadly bullet entered her head and she dropped to the ground. Then Mildred pointed the weapon to her own head. The bullet entered her brain and she fell unconscious.

Witnesses and neighbors rushed to the scene after hearing the gunshots. They found both girls lying on the wet ground, gasping for breath with blood and brain matter oozing from wounds in their skulls. Doctors, the local police and the mayor were summoned. Dr. Chandler was placed in charge of Mildred, and he was shocked that she was still alive, despite the gunshot wound directly at her ear. According to his reports, it was rare for anyone to survive such a wound, and he could find only six cases in which the victims of such wounds survived. Oddly, Mildred's appetite in the hospital was good, and she was quickly on the road to recovery. However, she carried the disfigurement of a twisted mouth for the rest of her life.

There wasn't enough room to accommodate everyone who showed up for Annie's funeral. Reverend J. Edward Wright officiated the services, and according to reports, he did all he could do to soften the sorrow of the family. Jack Wheeler was in attendance and was nearly inconsolable as he listened to the preacher commit Annie's lifeless form to the earth and her soul to the care of "its great Creator."

The courtroom was packed with spectators who possessed a "morbid curiosity." Mildred sat in a plush rocking chair, which she swung back and forth in while looking nervously around the room. It was revealed in court that Midred had visited a fortune-teller on Granite Street who told her that she was in trouble and that more trouble was in store for her. Witnesses described Mildred's erratic behavior in the days before the murder. The murder trial came to a conclusion in May 1898, when Mildred was found not guilty by reason of insanity.

She was committed to the State Hospital for the Insane in Waterbury. In 1908, she was released into the custody of Mrs. Ross, a family friend

The State Hospital building in Waterbury, Vermont, has been restored and is now used by state agencies.

who lived in Hardwick, despite the reservations physicians at the hospital had about her mental condition. Five months later, the order was revoked, and she was recommitted. The court documentation described her as a "degenerate" who could not "control her passions." Mildred had become infatuated with a young man in Hardwick, and she would not listen to the advice or warnings from Mrs. Ross.

Just eight years later, in 1916, Mildred made friends with some of the attendants at the state hospital. One of them petitioned the courts to become her guardian, and he took her to start a new life in Bellingham, Washington.

A field of wildflowers grows behind the row of maple trees at the edge of the Cutler Cemetery. The sun makes its way across the sky, warming the hillside graveyard throughout the day. The small gravestone for Annie faces the sunset, where, hopefully, her spirit peacefully journeyed into the light.

Oxbow Cemetery

Newbury

The spacious grounds of the Oxbow Cemetery along Route 5 in Newbury, Vermont, appear to be tranquil, with songbirds flying from the tree line at the edge of the grounds to perch on top of the gravestones. Under the pink granite gravestone of Orville Gibson lies a haunting mystery that has shadowed the town since 1957. The story of the "spilled milk murder," the gruesome death of Orville, has inspired folklore, songs and novels. There are many theories about what exactly happened on New Year's Eve 1957.

According to reports, it was just after 4:00 a.m. on December 31, when Orville went out to his barn to milk his cows—he never returned. When he didn't show up for breakfast in the morning, his wife, Evelyn, became quite concerned. She went out to the barn, but all she could find was an overturned pail and a trail of animal feed that led from the barn to the road. She ran back to the house and called the state police. After an extensive search by the authorities, there was no trace of Orville. Within hours of his disappearance, there was chatter in town that his disappearance may have been the result of vigilante justice.

In the weeks leading up to Orville's disappearance, there had been several angry exchanges between him and people he employed on the farm. Some of the men quit, while one man, Eri Martin, had a physical

The gravestone of Orville Gibson at the Oxbow Cemetery in Newbury, Vermont.

altercation with him on Christmas Day. The reason for the altercation was that Eri spilled two cans of milk in the barn. Orville was so angry that he allegedly gave the man a black eye, five cracked ribs and a bruised leg. The townspeople who had been filled with holiday cheer were now rattled and disgusted by what happened. Orville was supposed to appear in court on January 7 to face an assault charge.

It wasn't until March 26, 1958, that the fate of Orville Gibson was discovered. His body was pulled from the nearby Connecticut River; it had been bound and tied with rope. Over the previous three months, the state troopers had been working with the theory that the farmer was attacked and dragged off from his barn. There was speculation that the body was thrown from the bridge that connected Newbury to Haverhill, New Hampshire. The autopsy revealed that Orville had no broken bones and had died of asphyxiation.

One theory that emerged was that Orville's death was the result of suicide and that he had tied himself up to fake a murder. However, the police were not convinced, as they maintained that his hands were tied behind his knees so securely that they held for three months, even after being tossed in the swift river current. Also, he was wearing his farm clothes, and no baggage or money was found on him.

Surprisingly, a popular school janitor named Robert Welch and Frank Carpenter were arrested and brought to trial for murder. Eighty-four community members were brought in to take lie-detector tests before the trial was underway. The case brought before the court was circumstantial, and the charges were based on gossip from a drinking party, which was described by some as "a lynching party." The case against Welch was thrown out. The state produced about twelve witnesses, many of whom found themselves totally confused or became extremely hostile under cross-examination. Despite the efforts of the prosecution, there wasn't enough evidence to convict Frank Carpenter, and he was found not guilty. From coast to coast, the results of the court proceedings garnered headlines, and even more speculation.

The *Burlington Free Press* reported on March 11, 1960, that Orville's mother, Alice, made pleas to know who had murdered her son. She was quoted as saying, "I pray and pray. Will I live long enough to know?" Orville's parents never got their wish; they passed away while waiting for someone to come forward with more information that could solve the case. To this day, the case remains open and unsolved. However, every few years, the story is resurrected, as there are so many haunting questions: Was his death the result of revenge? Was there a cover-up? Could it truly have been a suicide? Inquiring minds still ask if there is even anyone left alive who knows the truth. Ultimately, the full story lies in Orville's grave in Newbury, Vermont.

BARRE CEMETERIES

Before the town of Barre even had its name, there was an ambitious, independent spirit beating in the hearts of its early settlers. These strong feelings and opinions clashed in an unforgettable fight between two men on September 3, 1793. Captain Joseph Thompson and Jonathan Sherman had a physical fight at a town meeting that was held to decide the town's name. The dispute was settled with a fistfight in Calvin Smith's barn. As the men vigorously assaulted each other, they fell to the hemlock floor; they rolled around until Sherman declared as he rose to his feet, "There, by God, the name is Barre." The next day, Sherman went to Dr. Robert Paddock to have the hemlock splinters removed from his "posterior." Later that day, the two men came together at a meeting to make the town name official. It came down to the person who gave the most money to build the meetinghouse. Ezekiel Dodge Wheeler offered "sixty-two pounds lawful money," and he declared the town's name would be Barre.

That same year, the citizens voted for "two burying grounds to be located on the north and south side of the Jail Branch." After some challenges and reconsideration, final decisions were made. In 1816, the Elmwood Cemetery was established, and the town purchased a piece of land at the back of the cemetery for $150 from the widow of Ezekiel Wood. The bodies from the Trow-Cobble Hill Cemetery were moved to join those from the congregation in Elmwood. The cemetery was expanded again in 1854.

Dr. Robert Paddock died at the age of seventy-four in 1842, and he was buried at the Elmwood Cemetery. The inscription on his stone says "that he was a valued physician of this town forty-nine years." Dr. Paddock is also remembered for an unusual event that occurred at the Congregational church. The deacons at the parish refused to permit the funeral of a nonmember at their church. According to the story, Dr. Paddock and his good friend Judge Chapin Keith were angry about the situation, so they each grabbed an axe and headed to the church at the hour of the funeral. They were met at the door by the deacons of the church, who, on seeing the determined faces of Dr. Paddock and Judge Keith and the weapons they carried, surrendered the key to the church. Then the funeral went on but with the declaration from the deacons that they had done their part in protecting the church and that all responsibility thereafter rested on the shoulders of the invaders. The funeral went forward without any incident or issue.

Also buried in Elmwood is Mrs. Lucy Whitney Wood, and her marble gravestone reads that she died on January 31, 1893, at the age of 107 years and 25 days old. According to newspaper articles, she lived a happy and healthy life and spent her centenarian days sewing, knitting, crafting quilts and greeting visitors. Her award-winning quilts comprised upward of six thousand individual pieces. She was born in Jaffrey, New Hampshire, and moved with her parents to Sterling, Massachusetts, and then to Milford. She met and married John Wood, and they lived in a log cabin with no doors or windows. They used blankets made of animal skins to keep out the cold, and she kept fires going all night to scare away wandering bears and wolves.

John served in the War of 1812, and the house the couple lived in caught fire twice. Lucy was alone in the house during one fire, and she permanently burned her hand while saving her infant daughter, Celinda, from the flames.

At the Evergreen Cemetery in Barre, an Egyptian-style sarcophagus and mourner can be found on the grave of the McLeod family.

She was described as a pioneer woman who was a living link to a distant past. She had ten children, and she celebrated her 107th birthday just weeks before her death. It was recounted that she entertained strangers, friends and family with a charming grace that was worthy of a queen at court.

Consisting of sixty-five acres in Barre, Hope Cemetery was established in 1895. The original architectural plan for the cemetery was designed by Edward P. Adams, a nationally known landscape architect. The careful planning and high architectural standards of the Hope Cemetery reflect the most progressive principles in cemetery design and development. The *Boston Globe* called the cemetery "one of the country's most astonishing collections of nostalgic statuary." For some people, the cemetery is a tribute to the melting pot of immigrants who left Europe with their families to start a new life in the Green Mountain State. Barre became known around the world for its master granite craftsmen, and many of these talented stone carvers were of Italian descent.

The large entryway of the cemetery invites visitors to enter and explore all of its impressive statues, memorials and monuments. The figures at the

Elia Corti's sculpture depicts stonecutters' tools at his feet among numerous other unique details.

entrance represent peace and salvation. Some of the memorial statues are incredibly lifelike, such as that of stone-carver Elia Corti. This piece stands almost eight feet tall, with a figure seated in front of a roughhewn boulder, his elbow on one knee and his fist resting next to his cheek, and at his feet is a palm leaf and stone-carving tools. This finely detailed sculpture was carved by his brother William and his brother-in-law, John Comi.

The story of Corti's death shocked the community of Barre. According to the *Barre Daily Times* on October 5, 1903: "He was shot in the stomach and mortally wounded, at a meeting in the socialist building on Granite Street and Alexander Garetto, a blacksmith, was arrested soon after, charged with the shooting. Corti died at midnight last night at the Heaton Hospital in Montpelier, having had lived about 30 hours after he received the bullet."

There were tensions between two groups in Barre between the pre–World War I anarchist and socialist factions. Corti, the editor of a socialist newspaper from New York City, was going to speak at the Socialist Hall. While people waited for his arrival, the shooting occurred. In December 1903, Garetto was tried and convicted of manslaughter, and he was sentenced to ten to twelve years of hard labor at Windsor Prison.

When Elia Corti's remains were brought by hearse to the Hope Cemetery, fifty-two wagons followed in succession up the hill. According to local folklore, the ghost of Elia was seen on Christmas Eve 1903, the same night Garetto was sentenced, near the Robbie Burns statue. The statue was erected by Scottish immigrants to commemorate the memory of the Scottish poet. Elia had created the intricate carvings on the base of the statue. The ghost of Elia was described as having his head down, looking at the monument as the snow fell around him.

Barre declares itself the "granite capital of the world"—and for good reason. Since the first granite quarry opened in Barre in 1810, Barre granite was deemed to be of the highest standard and was requested for sites all over the world. Initially, hand tools, such as hammers and iron wedges, were used to quarry the stone. The light gray granite found in Barre was used to build the state house in Montpelier, as well as the many works of memorial art at Hope Cemetery. The Rock of Ages quarry in Barre is the world's largest granite quarry. It is two miles wide and four and a half miles long, and it has enough granite to last for over four thousand years of coring at a depth of six hundred feet. It's been estimated that one-third of all the tombstones in the United States are made of Barre granite.

There have been six thousand deaths associated with the quarry due to accidents and, ironically, a lung disease called tuberculosis-silicosis. This fatal ailment was caused by the granite dust that was generated in the process of stone carving. Many of the stone-carvers and granite artisans buried at Hope Cemetery were taken prematurely to their graves because

Above: The Cassovoy grave marker at Hope Cemetery features a woman waving to a man riding a motorcycle.

Left: The sculpture over the Columbo grave at Hope Cemetery dates to 1905.

Opposite: The racecar gravestone sculpture of Armand Laquerre at Hope Cemetery in Barre.

of their trade. Vermont's cold climate made it necessary for the stone-carver to work indoors in poorly heated sheds with little ventilation. Ironically, about 70 percent of the artists and carvers designed their own tombstones, which can be found here. Many of their stones have no date of birth or death, just their name.

The fine detail of the monuments and markers is quite astonishing. Many of the monuments depict the hobbies or the profession of the person buried. Some stones have 3-D relief carvings of flowers delicately etched in granite.

There are a lot of fantastic monuments to discover, including a pair of pyramids, an airplane, an oversized soccer ball and a six-foot-tall letter "A." The grave of William and Gwendolyn Calvosa is a life-sized granite bed. A man and a woman are depicted sitting up in the bed in their pajamas, holding hands, their tombs stretched out before them. A set of connected wedding rings can be found on the grave of Janice Lee Stacey. Inside the rings is a portrait of a couple, a stag, children, a steaming pie and what appears to be warm brownies. There is also a striking, almost lifelike racecar on the grave of Armand Joseph Laquerre III, who died at the age of twenty-seven in 1991 in a snowmobile accident.

Above: The monument of William and Gwendolyn Halvosa depicts them sitting up in bed, holding hands.

Left: The "Bored Angel" at Hope Cemetery in Barre, Vermont.

The monument known as the *Dying Man* was designed to show a man dying of tuberculosis-silicosis. Louis Brusa started the carving in 1937 for himself and died later that same year. The woman cradling the sculpted man is supposed to be Brusa's wife, but local legend alleges that she looks more like his mistress. There is even the odd rumor that the shapely backside of the woman was found to be offensive and too racy for some in town.

Another monument with the Brusa name prominently carved on it is the *Bored Angel Statue*. Between two pillars, a curly-haired angel sits, staring into the distance. This sculpture was carved by Louis Brusa for his parents' grave. An ill, elderly woman with failing eyesight told her story about visiting the monument with her children. She felt deeply moved by visiting the Brusa angel. A few weeks later, one of her children reached out to the cemetery tour guide to say that she believed the angel miraculously helped to restore her mother's vision.

There is such a variety of unique memorials at Hope Cemetery, and it is impossible to include them all here. From the giant "Z" reminiscent of the Superman "S" shield to several different versions of praying angels and other pieces of religious iconography, this dazzling museum in stone warrants a thorough exploration. There is a lot of history to learn here from the monuments and memorials, like the memorial stone for the Spanish flu of 1918. Truly, this is not just a cemetery and garden of memorial stones; it is an art museum. It is easy to see why people from around the world come to visit this spectacular, sacred place.

SHARD VILLA MAUSOLEUM

Salisbury, Vermont

In what was described as a grim and singular token of Columbus Smith's character, the mausoleum at Shard Villa on the Salisbury Plains holds a lifetime of compelling stories. Irving Bacheller was a tutor to the Smith children, and he was quoted as saying, "In all the world, I think that there was not another man like Columbus Smith, or any other estate like his. He was the most picturesque figure of a man that ever stood before me—stout and of medium stature, thick hair, white as snow, eyes, and eyebrows black. As I remember him, there was not a wrinkle in his big, ruddy, smooth, serious

Left: The elegant Shard Villa mansion in Salisbury, Vermont.

Below: The Shard Villa mausoleum contains the bodies of Columbus Smith and his wife and children.

face. In it was the expression of indomitable will. One may almost say it was a will which had done impossible things."

Soon after Smith graduated with his law degree from Middlebury College in 1842, his pursuits led him to England. He was successful in helping people obtain their inheritances from long-lost relatives. When news of his accomplishments traveled, his client list and fortunes grew quickly. The case that brought Columbus the most notoriety was the settlement of the Francis Mary Shard estate in England. After spending fourteen years on the case, his tenacity paid off, with the estate being settled for $300,000, one-third of which became his fee for a job well done. Inspired—and as a tribute to Francis Mary Shard—he drafted plans for his estate Shard Villa in Salisbury.

The estate was going to be home to Columbus; his wife, Harriet; and his children, William and Mary. The mansion was built from native limestone, and the beautiful gardens were designed by an English gardener. A herd of buffalo was brought in to roam the estate's seven hundred acres. An Italian painter was brought in for two years to paint the elaborate frescoes and murals found throughout the mansion. There was one somber area of the house that remained simple and unadorned. In 1881, Smith's son, William, passed away from meningitis at the age of thirteen; his daughter, Mary, passed away from tuberculosis at the age of twenty-seven in 1897. The plain room in the mansion housed the memories of the deceased children without adornment, and Columbus and Harriet were completely heartbroken.

Just behind the mansion is an elegant Victorian mausoleum that was built in 1882 to house the earthly remains of Columbus and his family. The Smith children were interred in Victorian glass-top coffins inside. Also engraved on the mausoleum's door is the name Alexander Byrd McDowell and the date of his birth, November 23, 1866. He was the husband of Mary Smith for just one brief year before she died. Alexander was a doctor at the New York Infant Asylum, and he had gone on to be a clinical assistant. However, after his wife's death, he was quite despondent and died by suicide after he slashed his own throat in 1908. When his body was discovered, there was a picture of his dead wife, Mary, near his hand. Oddly enough, he was never interred in the mausoleum.

Columbus Smith was confined to one room of the mansion for four years, and he died of a heart attack in November 1909. Many people said that he was quite eccentric and had grown very delusional in his later years. Accusations about the mental state of Columbus also ran rampant for several years after his death, while his will was being processed through the courts.

He had made several modifications to the provisions of the will, including one that affected the future of the Shard Villa. His will stated that Shard Villa should be converted into a nursing home for "old Christian women not addicted to drink." Harriet Smith died in 1919, and the mansion was converted into a rest home, which it remains today.

The Smith family mausoleum behind the mansion can be seen from the road. There have been a few reports of a ghostly silhouette walking past the willow tree near the mausoleum entrance. This is believed to be the spirit of Columbus Smith looking over the grandeur of his visionary estate and his final resting place.

Old Joe, The Indian Guide

Newbury

Time dims the gaze, but the heart can see,
and the drum's swift beat sends the old man's feet
Flying down roads of memory.

The legends that surround folk heroes can be complex and can change with the telling of the tale over time. One gravestone in the Oxbow Cemetery in Newbury, Vermont, perhaps best tells people how to remember the man buried there.

Erected in memory of Old Joe
he Friendly Indian Guide
who died February 19, 1819

Old Joe was born into the Mi'kmaq tribe in Nova Scotia, Canada. When the British attacked Lewisburg in 1745, Old Joe fled to Quebec, Canada, where he was raised by the Saint Francis Abenaki people. He married an Abenaki woman known as Molly, and they lived a nomadic life. Traveling throughout Vermont during the French and Indian War, Joe warned settlers about impending raids. Joe also worked as a scout for General Jacob Bailey of Newbury during the American Revolution. Joe's skills were used to help map out the road that connected the Connecticut River Valley with Canada. It was quite an honor for him when a letter

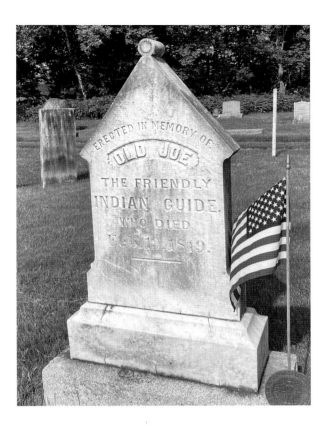

The gravestone for Old Joe, the "Indian guide" in Newbury, Vermont.

of appreciation arrived from George Washington with an invite to his headquarters along the Hudson River in Newburgh, New York. The journey required traveling by canoe and on foot. When he arrived, Washington shook his hand and invited the couple to an officers' dinner. According to the story, it was Joe's favorite memory.

Joe and Molly had two sons, and Joe was granted a pension from the state, which was increased as time passed to eighty-six dollars a year. As Joe grew older, some stories say that he enjoyed drinking rum so much that a series of guardians was appointed to help take care of him. In February 1819, Joe was out hunting on a cold winter night when both of his feet froze. A search party found him, and he died some days later. At his request, he was buried in the standing position, surrounded by his tomahawk, bow and arrows. He was given a military funeral, with shots fired over his grave.

A pond in West Danville, Vermont, was named after Joe, and the pond was described as a silver star set in a rug of deep green velvet. In Cabot, Vermont, a pond was named after Molly. In the 1950s, sewing kits to make

Joe and Molly dolls were sold by a gift shop in West Danville. A set of these dolls is in the collection of the Vermont Historical Society.

Joe was so revered by the people of Vermont that many continue to make sure his grave is properly marked with a suitable memorial: "For the friendly Indian guide who stood shoulder to shoulder with the Green Mountain Boys at the birth of a nation." While the spirit of this man is woven into the history of Vermont, there are some who say you may catch a glimpse of his spirit wandering the Oxbow Cemetery. Whether the presence of his ghost is real, it is undeniable that the people of Vermont will not let him be forgotten.

Green Mount Cemetery

Montpelier

On September 15, 1855, Green Mount Cemetery in Montpelier, Vermont, was dedicated. Charles G. Eastman wrote the following hymn the night before the dedication:

> *The fairest spot of hill and glade,*
> *We're blooms, the flower in waves the tree,*
> *And silver streams delight the shade,*
> *We consecrate, O Death, to thee.*
> *Here all the months of the year may know,*
> *Shall watch this "Eden of the Dead,"*
> *To wreathe with flowers or crown with snow*
> *The dreamless sleeper's, narrow bed.*
> *And when above its graves we kneel,*
> *Resigning to the memory moldering urn*
> *The friends whose silent heart shall feel*
> *No balmy summers glad return;*
> *Each marble shaft, our hands may rear,*
> *To mark where dust to dust is given,*
> *Shall lift its chiselled column here,*
> *To point our tearful eyes to heaven.*

The cemetery was established during the years the rural garden cemetery design brought the burial of the dead to scenic pastoral and beautifully landscaped places. The terraces and curves of the ground complement the land's lanes and the pathways. It seems as though around every corner, there is something else to discover: a beautifully carved figure, a handsome monument and a life story waiting to be told. The forty acres that became the cemetery were purchased from Isaiah Silver for $2,210. During the cemetery's dedication, Reverend F.W. Shelton eloquently described the location:

We stand upon a hillside, which almost yesterday, lay unreclaimed in its original wildness, and now already it begins to look like an embellished garden. Art has redeemed it from its rude estate, with an almost magic transformation. It has its winding walks, and will have its shady avenues. It is the most choice position in this valley, and its natural surface presents the charm of great variety. There is no stretch of landscape, in this neighborhood, around the abodes of the living, which can vie in beauty with this Paradise, which you now dedicate, as the resting place of your beloved dead. And it is easy to predict what its aspect will be in a few years, when it's remaining roughness shall have been assuaged; When every returning summer shall bring with it, a richer, shadow, and an added bloom—when affection shall have beautified it in every nook and watered its flowers with tears.

An older cemetery could be found on Elm Street in town, but the decision to move its remains to the Green Mount Cemetery was approved. A reflection on that move was also described during the dedication ceremony:

On the border of that village there is already a cemetery of the dead, but it would soon be overcrowded. It clamors already for a larger domain. Thus necessity itself has coincided with feeling in selecting a more ample and eligible place. There are many tender and touching associations, no doubt, connected with that spot, for its consecration is coeval with the settlement of this village. How many tears have fallen on its hither to [sic] untroubled and quiet graves. There the child, slumbers, and the young man, cut down in the nobility of his strength; there the blossoms of the almond tree have fallen; there the lovely daughter has been borne away, when bursting into the grace of womanhood, and when consumption like a worm to the bud, preyed on her damask cheek! There, truly, are deposited the richest treasures which you had on earth. But, if, in love and tenderness, you shall disturb those ashes, to bring them here, it will be only as when one shall rearrange a

Above: A carved angel in mourning can be found at the Bennett plot in Green Mount Cemetery.

Opposite: A carved loyal companion waits on top of a grave at Green Mount.

couch, that they may rest more sweetly and securely and quietly forever.

The first burial on the grounds was that of Simeon Lyman, a merchant, who was buried on October 3, 1855. He was forty-five years old at the time of his death. In the years that followed, almost all of the original cemetery commissioners, the pastor and the poet who wrote the hymn, were also buried here. Some of those who wandered the cemetery in the nineteenth century referred to their visits as trips to see old friends.

A granite bench sits under a cluster of trees in memory of Daniel Pierce Thompson, who died at the age of seventy-two in 1868. He was a graduate of Middlebury College and was a state legislator, probate judge and, later, secretary of state. He was also the editor of the antislavery *Green Mountain Freeman* newspaper, and he founded the Vermont Historical Society. The author of many books, he wrote the histories of Montpelier and the Green Mountain Boys.

There are also several Civil War Medal of Honor recipients buried here. U.S. senator and U.S. District Court judge Samuel Prentiss was buried under a towering obelisk. One of his many accomplishments was sponsoring a law banning dueling in the District of Columbia. Thomas Waterman, a world-class fine artist, was buried with his wife, Minerva. Their monument features bronze portraits of the couple and an artist's palette with brushes. A lifelike stone statue of a dog stands on the grave of Harry Edward "Ned "Stevens, who died from cancer in 1894. The symbolism of the dog is meant to remind visitors of faithfulness. The inscription reads: "Ned, only Child of Fred R. and Hattie E. Stephens, May 19, 1875–January 2, 1894. 18 beautiful years."

Toward the front of the cemetery are what are sometimes referred to as the "stairs to nowhere" or the "stairs to heaven." Carved into the stone is

Stowell Burial Place
Ledge work commenced June 19, 1897.
Completed November 3, 1898
Cut by Charles P Bailey

December 18, 1840–September 14, 1911
A Vermont craftsman.
Who served his trade
And his nation well
Granite Cutter and
Union Army Veteran
Of the Civil War
1861–1864
Great Grandfather of
Marilyn F Jillson

The stairs were hand carved with just a hammer and chisel into the existing blue-gray ledge. A large tablet lists the details of the Stowell family. Duren Stowell had selected this particular spot for his family to be buried in. He was born in Acworth, New Hampshire, and died at the age of eighty-five from heart disease in 1885. He was a superintendent of the Montpelier and Wells River Railroad.

At the southwest corner of the cemetery is a life-size stone sculpture of a young girl standing at a wooden gate. The details on this sculpture are so finite that the girl truly seems to be alive, and you might just catch a gleam in the eye of this beautiful child. The sculpture is often referred to as "Little Margaret." In 1899, Margaret Caroline Pitkin died at the age of seven from spinal meningitis. Margaret's parents contracted a local sculptor to render a statue in her image. In the photograph the sculptor was given, one of the buttons was missing on her boot, and it is rendered the exact same way on the sculpture. Her lacy dress, tiny necklace, ring on her finger and pinned pocket watch are carved with the precision of a true artist. At Margaret's feet are beautifully carved lilies and roses. If you look carefully when visiting, you may notice pennies tucked into areas of the sculpture. Legend says that each penny is a wish for Little Margaret's happiness. She inspired the 1985 song "Song for Margaret" by Dan Lindner (Banjo Dan), which tells her story.

John E. Hubbard was the wealthiest resident of Montpelier during the late nineteenth century. There was some controversy surrounding him, because his aunt Fannie Hubbard Kellogg left her fortune to the City of Montpelier. Her wish was to have some of that money used to build a library for the town and a chapel and gate for the Greenmount Cemetery. John contested her will and obtained her fortune. He decided that in time, he would donate the 134-acre park in the city that bore his name, along with the land for the Kellogg Hubbard Library and the Gothic chapel vault at the front of the cemetery. He died at the age of fifty-two after a long illness, which newspaper accounts said he bravely faced, in 1899. Former governor William Paul Dillingham, one of the executors of his will, commissioned Karl Bitter to create the sculpture of a young man's thoughts on death. This massive sculpture, which can be seen from quite a distance, is very dramatic and has inspired a ghostly legend that has been passed on for years. Referred to by many as "Black Agnes," the rumor says that anyone who dares to sit in the statue's lap at midnight will be cursed. There were stories of teenagers who allegedly broke their legs or even died as a result of the frightening curse. However, there is no documentation to prove that anyone actually died as a result of coming into contact with the statue. So, where did the legend come from?

The inspiration for the sculpture came from a similar sculpture called *Grief* at the Rock Creek Park in Washington, D.C. An amateur sculptor named Felix Agnus decided to create his own version of the statue at the Druid Hill Cemetery in Baltimore, Maryland. The statue became known as "Black Agnes," or "Aggie," and teenagers would dare each other to sit on her lap. They later

Is the Hubbard grave cursed by a figure known as "Black Agnes"?

This beautifully rendered carving of a child dates to 1905.

claimed that bad things happened to them afterward. Word of the cursed statue traveled to Vermont and was applied to the statue at Green Mount. The inscription to the left of the monument reads: "Thou go not like the quarry slave at night, Scourged to his dungeon, and soothed by an unfaltering trust." On the right, the inscription reads, "Approach thy grave, like one who wraps the drapery of his couch about him, and lies down to pleasant dream."

Wandering the grounds of the Green Mount Cemetery, visitors will discover the original cold storage vault dug into the hillside, which would've been used in the winter when the ground was too frozen to dig graves. A section near the entrance is reserved for infants and young children, which is evident from the toys and mementos left on the graves.

As far as haunted tales here go, there are stories of visitors hearing footsteps behind them while walking the paths. Some curiosity seekers even claimed to have captured unusual light anomalies in pictures. In my many visits to the cemetery, I never encountered anything spooky or creepy myself. Of course, I do keep an open mind. I did see the grounds come to life in a different way, however, through unique sculptures, monuments and tender portraits that were alive with memories, stories and history.

EVERGREEN CEMETERY

New Haven

Taphephobia is the fear of being buried alive. Translated from Greek, it literally means "fear of graves." A depiction of this can be found in the Evergreen Cemetery, located in a little country farm town called New Haven, Vermont. The welcoming, well-maintained cemetery has one very strange anomaly in it that harkens back to the days of Edgar Allen Poe's story "The Premature Burial."

The grave of Dr. Timothy Clark Smith (1821–1893) stands out among the beautifully carved stones. Dr. Smith led a fascinating life that took him on adventures all around the world. He was also a schoolteacher and served as a clerk to the Treasury Department. After obtaining his doctorate degree in 1855, he became a surgeon in the Russian army. Later, he served as a United States consul to Russia in both Odessa and Galatz until 1883. Approximately ten years after his return to Vermont, Dr. Smith passed away on Halloween Night.

The Vermont newspaper the *Middlebury Register* reported that Dr. Smith "died suddenly" on Saturday morning at the Logan House, a hotel where he had been living. After breakfast, he walked out into the office and stood by the stove when he was "stricken." During the nineteenth century, there were many people who feared being buried alive because of stories from all around the world of people who were presumed to be dead and buried prematurely. Dr. Smith was afraid of sleeping sickness overtaking him

The zinc grave marker shaped like a coffin is on the grave of Lillis Hinman Waite at the Evergreen Cemetery.

and making him appear dead when, in fact, he'd still be living. Therefore, those in charge of his remains exercised caution to prevent him from being buried alive.

First, the burial was delayed for as long as possible to make certain he was dead. During this time, Smith's burial vault was built and overseen by his son Harrison T.C. Smith of Gilman, Iowa. The design of the vault offered stairs and a viewing window at the top of a glass shaft so that Dr. Smith's interred body could look out and passersby could look in. A second room was built for Dr. Smith's wife, Catherine.

Dr. Smith's grave is near the front of the cemetery, rising up on a low mound. Local legend tells us that upon looking in the window, you can still see the skeleton of Dr. Smith, and at his side are a hammer and chisel that he could use to dig himself out of the grave if need be. It was also said that Dr. Smith was buried with a bell in his hand so he could ring it should he wake from the dead. Viewing the interior of the grave is difficult today due to the condensation that has built up in the window and the moss that has grown from the inside corners of the window.

It is difficult to see into the window of the most curious grave in the Evergreen Cemetery in New Haven, Vermont.

The cemetery is a beautiful place to explore, with spacious rows of tall Victorian gravestones and a receiving tomb that is still intact at the edge of the grounds. There is even a working vintage water pump there. However, there are no sounds of a ringing bell or the sight of moving shadows inside the burial vault of Dr. Timothy Smith, so perhaps one can conclude that he had nothing to fear in the end.

5

NORTHWEST VERMONT

JERICHO CENTER CEMETERY

Jericho

"The Snowflakes and the Flowers"

On a moonbeam bright,
A snowflake white,
Slid down to the grey old earth;
Of companions fair
It found myriads there,
In that hour of Winter's birth.
A mantle we'll weave
For the flowers we grieve,
That have vanished from field and wood;
With a cover so warm,
Wrap each dainty form,
And each head with a fleecy hood.
So the snowflakes cried,
And made haste to hide
The flowers from the north-wind chill;
So when Springtime came,

She found the same
Sweet blossoms on meadow and hill.

—*Mary Estabrook Hale,* Vermonter *11 (1902)*
(Mary died in 1930 and was buried at the Elmwood Cemetery in Barre,
Vermont.)

I wouldn't change places with Henry Ford or John D. Rockefeller for all
their millions. I have my snowflakes.

—*Wilson Bentley*

Wilson Bentley was born in Jericho, Vermont, in 1865 on a quaint but hardworking farm. He was homeschooled by his mother, a former schoolteacher, and she helped him to cultivate his love of nature. He was quoted as saying, "It was my mother who made it possible for me, at fifteen, to begin the work to which I have devoted my entire life."

An image of the exhibit for Wilson Bentley at the Jericho Historical Society.

Young Bentley was dazzled by snowflakes—so much so that he built a "laboratory" in a bare, cold room of the family farmhouse to study them. His mother encouraged his curiosity by providing him with a microscope to examine and sketch snowflakes. Bentley would even take his rock collection outside and lay it out on the ground in the shape of snowflakes. He was fascinated with the formation of ice crystals, and he set up a space in the woodshed for further study so that the snowflakes wouldn't melt so quickly. Bentley's parents sacrificed and saved to buy him a camera that cost $100, an expensive commodity for a hardworking farm family at the time. The purchase of the camera allowed Bentley to document groundbreaking discoveries under the lens, which secured his devotion to the craft.

Out of the trillions of snowflakes that fall from the sky, he realized that no two exhibited precisely the same crystal formation. On January 15, 1885, he was the first person to photograph a single snowflake. Bentley also made the distinction between small snowflakes and large snowflakes and their growth patterns. Small snowflakes had more intricate designs and formations. He also explored more of nature's frosty mysteries with his camera. Frosted windowpanes, insects and cobwebs covered in morning dew, along with frozen blades of grass, all became subjects for his keen eye.

In 1898, Professor G.H. Perkins from the University of Vermont wrote an article for a scientific magazine after viewing Bentley's photographs. The story went far and wide, like a drifting snowflake, and Bentley became known across the country as the "Snowflake Man." In 1923, a letter to a woman named Charlotte Bean of Brooklyn, New York, explained the excitement Snowflake Bentley experienced when collecting samples to put under his microscope: "As usual, when good snowflakes are falling, I did not stop for dinner or anything else, though I had callers, and became ravenously hungry. What thrills you would have had, could you have been with me while at work and seen the new beauties in the original, under the microscope."

Snowflake Bentley's photographs, slides and documentation helped advance the study of meteorology around the world. In November 1931, his book *Snow Crystals* was published, featuring over 2,400 images of snowflakes, frost and dew. The book remains in print today and is a valuable resource when exploring his life's work. He never married and died from pneumonia as a result of catching a deathly chill while working at the age of sixty-six at the family farmhouse in Jericho.

He was buried on the hillside of the Jericho Center Cemetery, and his modest gravestone reads "Snowflake Man." Not far from the cemetery in Jericho is the Old Red Mill, a National Historic Site built in 1855. This

A snowflake memento is found on the grave of the "Snowflake Man," Wilson Bentley.

distinctive gristmill is home to the *Snowflake Bentley* exhibit, which features his camera, microscope, photographs and personal effects to help tell his story. Operated by the Jericho Historical Society, it is an unforgettable place to visit to get close to Bentley's life work. As the seasons change and the snow drifts and melts on the grave of Snowflake Bentley, one can't help but honor the man who revealed the hidden beauty in the frosty treasures that fall from the sky.

THE GORGE OF DEATH

Richmond

There are nearly three hundred cast aluminum green historical markers crested with the Vermont state seal all over the Green Mountain State. These markers provide a fascinating glimpse into the state's past. One side of the sign for the Huntington Gorge in Richmond tells the history of the scenic spot, while the other side tells of numerous tragedies that befell visitors to this location.

> *Site of Richmond's first grist mill and electric generating plant. By 1902, John Preston had built a grist mill here at Richmond's best waterpower site. It was operated continuously for a century, last of all by the Robinson family. The Richmond Light and Power Co. converted the mill in 1903 to*

generate the village's first electricity. Other 19th-century mills here included cider, wool carding, and cloth dressing, woodturning, and underclothing.

The other side of the sign tells a grim story: "Eighteen people drowned here between 1950 and 1994. Most were swimmers caught by treacherous and deceptive currents that pulled them over the falls or sucked them down to the bottom of pools." A list of names, ages and years follows on the sign.

As of this writing, more than twenty-five people have died in the gorge. On a hot summer day, many people have found their way to the edge of the gorge to cool off in its shimmering waters and rapidly moving falls. The roaring and churning sounds of the foamy lime green waters beckon people along the dirt paths to the steep ledges. There is a series of deep pools and shallow, rocky sections spread out over more than half a mile of the river. Many people who have jumped from the forty-foot-tall cliffs have found themselves pulled downstream by the rapid current. In 1992, a state police diver died trying to retrieve a body in the gorge. In some cases, rescue efforts

The informational sign, warning visitors of the deaths that have occurred at Huntington Gorge in Richmond.

A view into the deadly gorge in Richmond, Vermont.

are delayed by dangerous conditions and rescuers have to wait for the waters to recede. Bodies have been recovered after previously becoming lodged in the gorge's underwater caverns, rock walls and deep tunnels.

Despite the posted warning signs and no parking zones, it seems as though nothing keeps people away. Every few years, it seems like the gorge makes frightening headlines detailing terrifying rescue attempts or other woeful deaths. It seems that just one visit can have deadly results.

NORTH CEMETERY

Isle La Motte

Crossing onto the northernmost island of Lake Champlain is a sign that tells travelers this is where Samuel de Champlain first landed in 1609. The stunning beauty of Isle La Motte, its vibrant orchards, vineyards and dairy farms, attracts visitors to the landscape. The geology of the island is particularly notable, as it is part of the 480-million-year-old Chazzy Fossil Reef, and there are many fossilized creatures to be examined along the shoreline there. There were also a few quarries that operated on the island, including a black limestone quarry.

William Montgomery was a ship's captain who lived on Isle la Motte in the nineteenth century. On a cold December day in 1876, he was captaining the *General Butler*, a Stanley canal boat and cargo vessel built in 1862 in Essex, New York. He was bringing a load of thirty tons of marble to Burlington, along with his daughter Cora and her friend to go Christmas shopping. Little did they know, they were journeying into what would be known as the "100 year storm," which challenged them with eight-foot-tall waves. The storm pounded the boat, and according to newspaper accounts, it was a terrifying experience, one that the passengers were not equipped to survive.

> *When nearing the north end of the breakwater shortly after noon, the schooner's wheel gave way, and the vessel began to drift at the mercy of the wind and waves. She was slowly driven, southward, outside the breakwater, until a short distance past the centre, where she let go her anchor and dragged nearly up to the structure. A little way beyond the southern lighthouse she struck, and all hands made haste to land on the breakwater. So tremendous was the force of the water that with each wave, the schooner would actually be sent higher than the breakwater; and alternately sinking, each plunge in the trough of the sea, would seem to be the last. To land on the breakwater, the members of the party were obliged to jump from the schooner, when it was on the crest of the wave; in the undertaking required, a leap of some eighteen feet onto a mass of large, rough stones covered with ice.*
>
> *The party, though having so narrowly escaped a sudden, violent, death, or even now, in a far from enviable predicament. They were already drenched to the skin and chilled to the marrow; and so violent was the gale that almost every wave dashed over the breakwater, giving the unfortunate party a fresh drenching every moment. But help was at hand. At this juncture, Mr. James Wakefield, with the courage and humanity worthy of all praise, accompanied by one of his sons, rowed out to the breakwater and rescued the party from their perilous and unpleasant position.*

—Burlington Weekly Free Press, *December 15, 1876*

The group ended up in the parlor of a house on Battery Street. There, Dr. H.H. Langdon examined the exhausted passengers. After hours passed and warmth flowed through their bodies, they were deemed out of danger and indeed survivors.

Strangely, in July 1907, the schooner *William Montgomery* (believed to be owned at one time by captain William Montgomery) was carrying a load of lumber when it ran into troubles near the railroad bridge between North Hero and South Hero Islands. Captain John Fleury was trying to navigate against fiercely strong winds when the schooner was smashed against one of the piers and immediately sunk. The crew quickly escaped in lifeboats, and it took quite some time to clear the channel.

Captain William Montgomery died at the age of ninety on March 14, 1922, and he was buried at the North Cemetery at Isle la Motte. A funeral urn with a carved eternal flame tops his large grave marker. He was buried with his wife, Margaret, and several of their nine children. Amazingly, the schooner the *General Butler* is still resting on the bottom of Lake Champlain, near the breakwater, and today, it looks like a ghost ship, lost in time and covered with sea life. Inside is the load of marble, untouched for over one hundred years. This incredible artifact, hidden from view, reminds us of the terrifying experience of Captain William Montgomery and the danger he faced during that December storm.

EAST CEMETERY

Williston

A crumbling gravestone in the East Cemetery in Williston, Vermont, says that Sally Griswold was "massacred" in August 1865. The views across the Champlain Valley from Sally's Juniper Hill Farm were nothing short of spectacular. She was said to be a cranky, disagreeable woman; however, she had worked hard her entire life to obtain what she had. Sally had lost each of her four children before they reached the age of eighteen months. Adelia Potter was Sally's adopted daughter from her sister Elihu. Adelia and her husband, Charles, moved back and forth between Canada and Vermont to avoid creditors, and eventually, they moved onto Sally's farm to help out. While they were helping out, they came up with a plan to move Sally off the property and take over the farm. Sally had no intention of leaving; however, Adelia and Charles attempted to have her declared insane. Their scheme to have Sally locked away in an asylum was unsuccessful.

Charles had a friend in New York whom he contacted to arrange a murder. A man named John Ward traveled by train to Burlington to discuss the details. After a few more meetings, an agreement was made, and the plans were set. Charles and Adelia packed up and headed to Canada to establish an alibi. To make it easier for John to do the dark deed, Charles filed the front door latch to the farmhouse to make an easy entry for John on the night of the murder. John had a plan to execute, and once he arrived, he barred the room where Sally's thirteen-year-old farmhand was sleeping. He then slipped into the house through the door that had the filed latch. He didn't expect Sally to be

The grave of Sally Walker is carved with the word *massacred*.

awake. According to the story, John attacked Sally, and she fought back as he violently stabbed her in the face, eventually cutting her throat. The community was shocked at the heinous crime, and it was uncertain at first if the murderer would ever be found. Someone had seen Ward shortly after the incident with blood on his clothes. A local private detective was able to put together a motive and leads connected to New York City. John Ward still had to collect payment for the job, so three weeks later, he headed back to the Burlington area. He was arrested before he stepped off the train.

The case went to a trial, in which both Charles Potter and John Ward were charged. The trial was called sensational for its day. The testimony included the grisly evidence of bloody footprints that were found at the scene. John Ward was sentenced to death. While he did conspire with Charles to escape, he never got the chance. He was confined in prison for approximately thirteen years. It was said that he ate and slept well while incarcerated. On the day of Charles's execution, two ministers from Saint Albans shared their spiritual advice with John. Said to have been reconciled to his fate, he appeared fearless and without conscience before the gallows. As John stood on the scaffold, he said, "Now, as I am to appear before God, I humbly state what is true. I neither struck nor injured the old lady. Her blood is not on my hands, although I knew, and in fact, participated in the murder. If that constitutes murder, then I'm a murderer." The fifty witnesses watched the platform as John dropped four feet from the hangman's noose to his death.

Charles and Adelia Potter were convicted of having burglar's tools; Charles was sentenced to ten years in prison, and Adelia was sentenced to seven years in state prison. Adelia died at the age of forty-two from a brief illness she contracted in jail. Charles was eventually pardoned by Governor Fairbanks, and he left Vermont and headed west. Sally's gravestone is a reminder of the horror that occurred one night in 1865 in the peaceful town.

THE HIBERNATION OF HUMAN BODIES IN THE SNOW DRIFTS OF WASHINGTON COUNTY

A story printed on page 9 of the *Rutland Daily Herald* on May 24, 1939, perhaps caused people to wonder what—or who—might be lingering in the melting snow drifts in Washington County after a long, cold Vermont winter. The article referred to a newspaper clipping that was found in an old scrapbook owned by Elbert S. Stevens of Bridgewater Corners. The clipping tells the story of an unnamed traveler who became a witness to a strange ritual that shook him "to the roots of his soul." The traveler's story is shared by "A.M.," who claimed that it was copied from the diary of his "Uncle William." He vouched for the story's authenticity, as he claimed to have spoken directly to a man who faintly remembered the disturbing events of that time. The clipping from the diary (reprinted in its entirety in the *Rutland Herald*) read as follows:

> *The account runs in this wise. January 7: I went on the mountain today, and witnessed to me what was a horrible sight. It seems that the dwellers there who are unable, either from age or other reasons, to contribute to the support of their families, are disposed of in the Winter months in a manner that will shock the one who reads this diary, unless that person lives in that vicinity. I will describe what I saw. Six persons, four men and two women, one of the men a cripple about thirty-years old, the other five past the age of usefulness, lay on the earthy floor of the cabin, drugged into insensibility, while members of their families were gathered about them in apparent indifference. In a short time the unconscious bodies were inspected by several old people, who said, "They are ready." They were then stripped of all their clothing, except a single garment. Then the bodies were carried outside, and laid on logs, exposed to the bitter cold mountain air, the operation having been delayed several days for suitable weather.*

It was night when the bodies were carried out, and the full moon, occasionally obscured by flying clouds, shone on their upturned, ghastly faces, and a horrible fascination kept me by the bodies as long as I could endure the severe cold. Soon the noses, ears and fingers began to turn white, then the limbs and face assumed a tallowy look. I could stand the cold no longer, and went inside, where I found the friends in cheerful conversation.

In about an hour I went out and looked at the bodies; they were fast freezing. Again I went inside, where the men were smoking their clay pipes, but silence had fallen on them; perhaps they were thinking of the time when their turn would come to be cared for, in the same way. One by one they at last lay down on the floor and went to sleep. It seemed a horrible nightmare to me, and I could not think of sleep. I could not shut out the sight of those freezing bodies outside, neither could I bear to be in darkness, but I piled on the wood in the cavernous fireplace, and, seated on a single shingle block, passed the dreary night, terror-stricken by the horrible sights I had witnessed.

January 8: Day came at length, but did not dissipate the terror that filled me. The frozen bodies became visible, white as the snow that lay in the huge drifts about them. The women gathered about the fire and soon commenced preparing breakfast. The men awoke and, conversation again commencing, affairs assumed a more cheerful aspect. After breakfast the men lighted their pipes, and some of them took a yoke of oxen and went off towards the forest, while others proceeded to nail together boards, making a box about ten feet long and half as high and wide. When this was completed, they placed about two feet of straw in the bottom; then they laid three of the frozen bodies on the straw. Then the faces and upper part of them were covered with a cloth, then more straw was put in the box, and the other three bodies placed on top and covered the same as the first ones, with cloth and straw. Boards were then firmly nailed on the top, to protect the bodies from being injured by carnivorous animals that make their home on these mountains.

By the time the men, who went off with the ox-team, returned with a huge load of spruce and hemlock boughs, which they unloaded at the foot of a steep ledge; came to the house and loaded the box containing the bodies on the sled, and drew it to the foot of the ledge, near the load of boughs. These were soon piled on and around the box, and it was left to be covered with snow, which I was told would lie in drifts twenty feet deep over this rude tomb. "We shall want our men to plant our corn next spring," said a youngish-looking woman, the wife of one of the frozen men, "and if you want to see them resuscitated you come here about the 10ᵗʰ of next May."

With this agreement, I left the mountaineers, living and frozen, to their fate, and returned to my home in Boston, where it was weeks before I was fairly myself, as my thoughts would return to that mountain with its awful sepulchre.

Turning the leaves of the old diary to the date of May 10, the following entry was found:

May 10: I arrived here at 10 A.M., after riding about four hours over muddy, unsettled roads. The weather is warm and pleasant, most of the snow is gone, except here, and there drifts in the fence corners and hollows, but nature is not yet dressed in green. I found the same parties here that I left last January, ready to disinter the bodies of their friends. I had no expectations of finding any life there, but a feeling that I could not resist impelled me to come and see. We repaired at once the well-remembered spot at the ledge. The snow had melted from the top of the brush, but still lay deep around the bottom of the pile. The men commenced work at once, some shoveling away the snow, and the others tearing away at the brush. Soon the box was visible. The cover was taken off, the layers of straw removed, and the bodies, frozen and apparently lifeless, lifted out and laid on the snow. Large troughs made out of hemlock logs were placed nearby, filled with tepid water, into which the bodies were separately placed, with the head slightly raised. Boiling water was then poured into the trough from kettles hung on poles near by, until the water in the trough was hot as I could hold my hand in. Hemlock boughs had been put in the boiling water in such quantities that they had given the water the color of wine. After lying in this bath about an hour, color began to return to the bodies, when all hands began rubbing and chafing them. This continued about another hour, when a slight twitching of the muscles of the face and limbs, followed by audible gasps, showed that life was not quenched, and that vitality was returning. Spirits were then given in small quantities, and allowed to trickle down their throats. Soon they could swallow, and more was given them, when their eyes opened, and they began to talk, and finally set up in their bathtubs. They were then taken out and assisted to the house, where, after a hearty dinner they seemed, as well as ever, and in nowise injured, but rather refreshed, by their long sleep of four months.

Truly, truth is stranger than fiction.

Could this story be true? Were people placed in an icy hibernation for the winter so as not to be a burden to their families? Was there some sort of science at work that the hill folk of Vermont had figured out in order to cheat death? This story eventually made its way into the Boston newspapers and has since been told far and wide by believers and skeptics alike.

Greenmount Cemetery

Burlington, Vermont

Born in Litchfield, Connecticut, in 1738, Ethan Allen purchased land in the New Hampshire Grants in 1770. He founded the Green Mountain Boys to protect against claims from New York that threatened the Vermont Territory during the American Revolution. The dramatic capture of Fort Ticonderoga from British soldiers in 1775 by Ethan Allen and Benedict Arnold was arguably one of the pivotal moments of the American Revolution. Ethan Allen had plans to attack Montreal, but he was captured by British soldiers and held on a prison ship for three years. He wrote about his experience in *A Narrative of Colonel Ethan Allen's Captivity* in 1779. When he returned to Vermont, he lobbied for the state's entry into the Union as the fourteenth state. He died from a stroke on February 12, 1789. There was some controversy about where he was buried, and an extensive article in the July 19, 1873 issue of the *Burlington Free Press* chronicled all the details.

About the year 1860, there was some controversy as to just where Ethan Allen was really buried. His resting place was marked by no tomb, though other members of his family were buried near together in the Green Mount Cemetery, here, and monuments had been placed over their graves. Competent judges determined that Ethan's grave must lie at or near this spot.

It is true that at the time of the erection of the present monument in Green Mount Cemetery a discussion arose as to where Allen was buried, but never was the opening of a controversy more uncalled for Allen's grave had for many years been marked by a horizontal stone of white marble, bearing the following inscription:

The Corporeal Part of
Genl. Ethan Allen
Rests beneath this stone
Who died the 12th day of Feb 1789
Aged 50 years
His spirit tried the mercies of his God.
In whom he believed and strongly trusted.

Within our recollection, the stone was perfect; but relic hunting vandals from abroad began to knock off small pieces to carry away with them, and

Ethan Allen is buried underneath this tall column at the Greenmount Cemetery in Burlington, Vermont.

at the time of the erection of the present monument but a small piece of it remained. There was no earthly reason to doubt the literal truth of the inscription as to the fact that Allen's body was buried beneath the stone. But it chanced that the excavation on the spot once covered by the stone, for the foundation of the present monument, failed to disclose a skeleton. Portions of a human skull and of other bones were found, the rest of the skeleton, doubtless, having decayed and mingled with the loose and sandy soil, which was not of a character to preserve for many years the remains committed to it. But there were not enough of the remains found to satisfy the expectations of some persons, who, thereupon, started the idea that perhaps, after all, Allen was not buried there. The matter was considered by the late George W. Benedict of consequence enough to warrant some time and labor, in setting the question at rest. He visited several witnesses of Allen's burial, then living in this vicinity, and from their affidavits, and from the position of the grave in relation to the adjacent graves of the Allen family, he demonstrated to the absolute satisfaction of every one who had cared to consider the proof, that Allen's grave was beneath the old stone. A paper presenting the evidence on the subject, prepared by him, is in the files of the Vermont Historical Society, and, we believe, is marked for publication in a future volume of the Society's collections. The doubt raised on the subject was very speedily allayed by the presentation of the evidence, and has had no resurrection since.

The current monument for Ethan Allen at Green Mount was constructed in two phases during the Civil War. Resting on an eight-foot-tall granite base with marble tablets, the thirty-five-foot-tall Doric column was constructed in 1858. The granite is believed to have been salvaged from the 1838 Vermont State House that previously burned down. In 1873, an eight-foot-tall Carrara marble statue of a young Ethan Allen in a pose demanding the surrender of Fort Ticonderoga was placed on top of the column.

Lakeview Cemetery

Burlington, Vermont

In 1867, the City of Burlington purchased twenty-three acres of land from H.B. Sawyer for the amount of $3,500 to establish a cemetery. Expanded further in 1868, the cemetery was designed as a garden-style park cemetery located at the end of the city's trolley line. The tranquil grounds, with a variety of trees like Colorado blue spruces and Japanese silk maples, were designed to be inviting. Overlooking Lake Champlain, the scenic spaces were perfect for Victorian picnics after visiting the graves of loved ones.

The spectacular Louisa Howard Chapel was built in 1882 in the high Victorian Gothic style. It is now in the National Register of Historic Places and is still used for certain public gatherings. Louisa's brother John built the beautiful fountains for the cemetery. Both Louisa and John Howard were involved in philanthropy and many community causes that made a difference for the residents of Burlington.

There are many interesting areas of the cemetery to explore, such as the small paupers' section, where there are several rows of gravestones with just numbers and no names. A life-size granite replica of a ski chalet can also be found with an amazing amount of fine details. There are two bronze doors, each with clear glass panels that seal the mausoleum area. Above each door are stained-glass windows that depict a man and a woman skiing on a snowy slope. Next to the door are his-and-hers granite skis. A bronze plaque on the structure tells the story of Chuck and Jann Perkins, who had an adventurous life and founded the Alpine Shop. The stone chalet was built to their specifications in 2005, while they were alive.

A statue of General George Jerrison Stannard can be found in the cemetery. The statue is complete in uniform with a cutlass at his side, and one can see that his right arm was amputated at the elbow, as the sleeve of the statue is pinned to the front of the uniform. The plaque on the statue tells of his Civil War experience: "At Gettysburg, July 3, 1863, commanding the 2nd VT brigade in the crisis of the battle, he made the flank attack which decided the fate of Pickett's charge and changed doubtful struggle into victory."

An area of the cemetery that evokes much sadness (and, according to local tours, the occasional ghostly experience) is a group of fifty-one small marble headstones. These children's graves have names like "Little Harry," "Baby Kirk," "Baby Ruth" and "Cora May Grey." A large granite marker with a cross stands nearby and reads:

Ereced by Louisa H. Howard
To the Memory of the Children
Who Have Died in the
Home for Destitute Children
Burlington, Vermont 1884

The gravestones were restored by a large group of volunteers who came from all over the state in September 2022. The children at the home who were buried here came from a variety of circumstances and backgrounds. Some of the children were orphans, others were neglected and some struggled

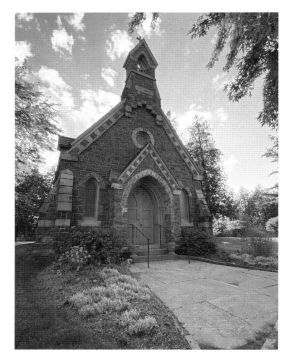

Left: The gothic chapel at Lakeview Cemetery in Burlington was built in 1882.

Below: The greek columns on the Austin grave at Lakeview Cemetery help to make the marker look like a gateway to Lake Champlain in the distance.

Above: Visitors to the graves of the children who lived in the orphanage claim that it can be a very spirited spot of the Lakeview Cemetery.

Right: The Perkins ski lodge mausoleum is one of the most unique structures at the Lakeview Cemetery.

with poverty or came from crisis situations. The unavailability of modern medicines and vaccines, along with a lack of good health maintenance, was a challenge for the children. Ailments like tuberculosis, diarrhea, diphtheria and scarlet fever were challenging to overcome in the late nineteenth century. These small stones are reminders that some of the youngest residents of Burlington had stories to tell, and they should not be forgotten.

A pair of fluted stone columns supporting a pediment bears the name "Austin" and looks like a gateway to the lake. Warren Robinson Austin was a lawyer who served as a U.S. senator for Vermont from 1931 to 1946, when he became an ambassador to the United Nations until 1953. There are many graves throughout the grounds for Civil War and military heroes. A small gravestone under shady trees can be found for Leander W. Freeman, who was seventy-six when he died in 1917. Leander served as a private in the Massachusetts Fifty-Fourth Colored Infantry. A flag waves next to the marble gravestone for Israel Freeman, who was twenty-eight when he died in 1872. He served as a private in the Forty-Third United States Colored Infantry. The stone was erected by the Stannard Post No. 2 GAR.

The grave for Urban Andrain Woodbury can be found here. He was a sergeant in the Civil War, a prominent businessman and, eventually, an elected officer and governor of Vermont. A granite marker on a three-tiered pedestal can be found for Philomene Pasha Lamoine (Cathey), who was a notorious madam who ran a busy brothel on Main Street in the late nineteenth century. While she had numerous run-ins with the law, she was viewed by many as a philanthropist who took care of those in need. A tall obelisk can be found for the Howard family, including Louisa and John, who were not only contributors to the legacy of the Lakeview Cemetery but were also permanent residents.

6

THE NORTHEAST KINGDOM

ALBANY VILLAGE CEMETERY

Albany

In the Albany Village Cemetery, you'll find the gravestones of the Hayden family, who died between 1837 and 1927. Just up the road is a handsome brick house that was built in 1854 once owned by the family. The creepy stories that surround this house offer hair-raising paranormal encounters and a generational curse from beyond the grave.

It was the early 1800s in Braintree, Massachusetts, when William Dale and his wife, Silence, left for Lutterloh (now Albany), Vermont. Recently widowed Mercy Dale, William's affluent mother-in-law, joined them. In time, William became a property owner and town selectman. Despite his success, he was overly ambitious and eventually ran into financial troubles. When he turned to Mercy for help in taking care of his debts, she flat-out refused to give him a dime. In fact, her health was failing, and she blamed him for poisoning her. The ill, old woman ended up in the care of a neighbor, and right before she died in 1808, she proclaimed her now-famous curse: "The Hayden name will become extinct in the third generation, and the last will die in poverty." She had also made it clear before she died that she did not want to be buried in the family plot in Albany. William continued making bad financial decisions and was on the run from creditors. He went

The Hayden family is buried at the Village Cemetery, just down the road from their mysterious house in Albany, Vermont.

to Canada for a time, but he ended up penniless and destitute in Farnshoile, New York, where he died in 1846.

His son William Jr. remained in Albany, Vermont. However, he wasn't any better with money. In 1854, William Jr. decided to build a glorious Greek Revival mansion, and he spared no expense. He ordered granite from the Barre quarries to be brought via oxcart to build the foundation for the house. He even had a spring-suspended dance floor constructed on the third floor. The dining room could seat thirty people, who were served with silver platters. There were even rumors that séances were held in the house in the hopes of reversing his grandmother Mercy's curse. Word around town said that he was reckless and liked to party even more than his father had. Two maids were employed at the house, which was described as being exquisitely furnished. William Jr. married Azubah Culver, and the couple had five children. The couple lost one child in childbirth, and they ended up having marital issues and became estranged. William Jr. suffered a stroke and struggled with partial blindness before he died in 1883 at the age of eighty-two.

The allegedly cursed Hayden House in Albany, Vermont.

Henry Williams's only surviving son had plenty of problems in his life as well. According to newspaper reports, Henry took underhanded steps to cheat family members out of their inheritances by burning important legal documents. He gambled away much of his money by betting on horses. There were suspicions that Henry smuggled Chinese immigrants from Canada to Connecticut, making use of the alleged tunnels under the family mansion. Some of the locals even believed that part of the family fortune may have been buried somewhere on the property.

In October 1910, a horse-drawn hearse clattered along South Albany Road, carrying the dead body of Henry to the Village Cemetery. Henry was the father of four children born to his wife Lydia; his only son, William Andrew, died at the age of five in 1871. His gravestone is located in the same row as his father's stone, and the epitaph reads: "Suffer little children to come with me and forbid them, not for such is the kingdom of heaven."

One of his twin daughters, Willimenia, died at the age of seventeen in 1891. His daughter Carrie died just one week before Henry passed. His daughter who lived the longest had an unfortunate story as well. To escape her family's unsavory reputation, she went back to her mother's hometown of Waterville, Maine. According to Mamie's obituary, she was "of a friendly disposition, clinging to her old friends with a closer tie than all people are inclined to do." After her passing in 1927 from a long illness, her body was returned to the family plot in Albany.

The Hayden mansion exchanged hands for a time, and it seemed plagued by several unfortunate accidents. Part of the mansion and its barns burned to the ground in what were called "mysterious fires." In an odd coincidence, one of the firemen who was on the scene, Mr. Mason, was stricken with polio two days after fighting the fire and was confined to a wheelchair for the rest of his life. During that time, it was rumored that the secret tunnels were being used for bootlegging. Finally, the house was abandoned by everyone, except for the thieves and vagrants, who broke in and stole whatever they could find.

Whispers of the old curse still echoed through the community, and stories of disembodied spirits inhabiting the house were commonplace. Orchestral music was described as emanating from the now-empty ballroom. A distant relative named David Meehan stopped by the house, but he didn't dare go inside. He went only as far as the porch. According to reports, two weeks later, David was in a car accident, and he ended up paraplegic. Apparitions of people dressed in nineteenth-century clothing have been seen in the windows on the property over the years.

The Hayden family plot can be easily found in the Albany Village Cemetery on Route 14, just up the road from the Hayden mansion. There are a few people who remember when the plot was surrounded by a cast iron fence and white marble lambs, all of which are gone today. Perhaps, even in their final resting place, the family couldn't escape Mercy Dale's curse.

The Dog Chapel

St. Johnsbury

A sign that reads "Welcome, All Creeds, All Breeds, No Dogmas Allowed" greets visitors at the Dog Chapel in Saint Johnsbury, Vermont. Just past the sign is a small chapel, not unlike many of the country chapels seen in the rolling hillsides of Vermont, but this one is different. A twenty-four-karat gold-leafed flying Labrador retriever weathervane can be found on the cupola of the church. The Dog Chapel is a memorial for long-gone pets, with photographs and personal notes covering the walls of this space that speaks of love and devotion. There are stained-glass windows with profiles of dogs on them. Even the benches were made in the shape of dogs.

This inspirational place was created by Vermont folk artist Stephen Huneck, who was motivated by a near-death experience after an injury. He described that the spirit of a dog had come to him when he was healing and inspired him to build the chapel. He was the author of several children's books, but a special book called *Dog Chapel* was published in 2002. It describes the chapel and the joy of the relationships that dogs have with humans. Stephen was a creative artist who produced whimsical works in several mediums, including sculpture, painting and print. Some of his work has been preserved in the Smithsonian Institution and at the Shelburne Museum in Vermont.

Stephen struggled with depression and died by suicide in 2010 at the age of sixty. His wife, who never fully recovered from his loss, also died by suicide in 2013. The Dog Chapel is still open, and Stephen's studio and gallery are still visited by travelers from all over the world. Many people bring their dog's ashes to be scattered on the hillside as they walk along the scenic trails surrounded by fields of wildflowers and peaceful streams. A nonprofit organization was formed to make sure the legacy and history of Dog Mountain and its unique chapel are carried on for generations to come.

VILLAGE CEMETERY

Peacham

A tall marble gravestone stands in the shade of a maple tree at the Village Cemetery in Peacham, Vermont. Across the top, it reads, "Erected by the Citizens of Peacham." The stone tells only part of the harrowing story of the snowstorm that occurred on the night of March 4, 1869. According to newspaper accounts, seventy-four-year-old Esther Emmons, her daughter Mary and eight-year-old grandson, Willie, left Marshfield to go to the house of Esther's sister, which was located in the extreme southern area of town. They attempted to make the arduous journey on foot, which proved to be quite troublesome. After traveling about six miles, they tried to find shelter, but it was said no one would take them in. A resident of the town offered to give the grandmother a ride, but she refused because he could not take the entire group, so they continued their fatal trek as the storm bore down on them.

The group had grown so exhausted that they kept sitting down to rest. It was noted that they went by Mr. Stewart's house in town at 5:00 p.m. After traveling another two miles, the group was exposed in the open countryside, where Esther fell down in the snow. Mary followed the roadside fence, still looking back at her mother in hopes of finding help, but she, too, was eventually stopped by the snowstorm. It was then up to little Willie to try to find help, and he headed toward a faint light he saw in the distance. The light was coming from the home of Frank Farrar. Willie was about forty feet away from the door when he shouted for help. The Farrar family heard noises outside the house, but they never went to see who it might be, and eventually, the sounds faded away. The next morning, all three were found frozen to death where they fell. Esther was found in the path about half a mile from the house, Mary was found underneath the fence and Willie was found on the path he made in the snow when trying to reach the house. The inscription on their gravestone reads "A Mother, Daughter and Grandchild who perished…having travelled on foot nearly 15 miles during the day."

7

UNEARTHING THE GHOSTS

GRAVE ROBBING AND THE HUBBARDTON RAID

The sun was just rising in the sky when three hundred men from Hubbardton gathered to make the five-mile walk to Castleton, Vermont. Leading the angry citizens was the local sheriff. Rumors had been circulating throughout the town that graves were being robbed. The proof had come just shortly before the dawn gathering. Mrs. Penfield Churchill had been buried on Saturday, November 20, 1830. The cemetery's sexton was on alert after Mrs. Churchill's burial, and he became quite suspicious of strange and illicit activity that kept happening at night, so he set a trap to confirm his hunch. He carefully arranged the graveside flowers in a specific manner after a particular burial, and he made a nearly invisible mark at the gravesite. He kept his eye on the grave, and a few days later, he discovered that the flowers had been displaced, and his mark was completely gone.

The sexton immediately informed the woman's husband and town leaders of his grim discovery. Groups of men showed up at the gravesite with shovels in hand, ready to dig down to the truth. Once the shovels clanked against the coffin, it emanated a hollow sound. The dirt was brushed away, and the coffin lid was raised. The suspicions were justified—the body was gone, and the coffin was empty. The belief was that the body had been taken to the Castleton Medical School for possible dissection.

The mob in Hubbardton carried clubs and weapons with them, and when they arrived at the school, they demanded to be let in. The dean of the school came up with a plan to delay their entry to the school by claiming he didn't have the key to the facility. He proceeded to send a student to his home to retrieve it. While all of that was going on, inside the school, the students cut the head off the body, hoping to conceal its identity. Some floorboards of the school were also pulled up to hide the body underneath. One student carried the head of the corpse underneath his cape and ran past the mob to a local hayloft to hide.

Finally, the key to the building was in the dean's hand, and the farmers and woodsmen looked everywhere for the remains of their neighbor. As they explored the school, they were disgusted and shocked at what they saw. They discovered that there were dissected human remains, including arms and legs, scattered about the rooms. The tools used by the students—knives, saws and forceps—were also visible. During the extensive search, a keen-eyed member of the mob discovered a section of the floorboard that had not been tacked down. The floor was torn up to reveal the headless body. The dean of the school insisted that if charges weren't levied against the school or students, he would produce the head. The head was brought back to the school by a student and reunited with the body. The remains were then finally laid to rest.

This incident became known as the Hubbardton Raid. John McNabb Currier penned a piece called the "Song of the Hubbardton Raid." The song was delivered at an oyster supper given by Dr. and Mrs. Sanford to the members of the Castleton Medical and Surgical Clinic on the evening of November 29, 1879. An excerpt follows:

In this ancient seat of learning,
In this house of dead flesh and bones,
Were set up long rows of tables,
Tables covered with human bodies,
Tables covered with stains of human blood,
Tables on watch for many years,
In this land of slate and quarries.
Around these tables, the dissected,
Dissected with the relish and love,
To learn the structures of the body,
To learn the different diseases,
In the town of green and purple slates.
Whoever died for miles around,
This numerous and savage class,
This class of savage students,

We're sure to adore these tables,
The flesh would feed the students fire,
In this land of slates and quarries.
The friends with deck, the graves,
Deck, the mounds of fragrant flowers,
And drop a tear over empty coffins,
Coffins rifled of their contents,
In this green mountain in Athens,
In this town of slate inquiries,
Quarries of green and purple slates,
Slates that never fade nor tarnish.

The building that was once used as the medical school has since been moved, and it is now called the old chapel at Castleton University. It is the oldest building on campus. The building has served many purposes over the years; however, many people have gone on record to say that it's haunted. In October 2019, a public ghost investigation took place at the old chapel. Students were present and participated. Even the university's newspaper covered the investigation, which concluded that there were seven different ghosts there. Are they the spirits of people whose bodies were stolen from their graves and dissected in the name of science in the early days of the building? We may never know for sure.

PLYMOUTH NOTCH CEMETERY

Plymouth

The gravestone of Achsa Sprague at the Plymouth Notch Cemetery in Plymouth, Vermont, depicts a hand holding a crown. The inscription tells visitors that she "Went Home," and the bottom of the stone reads, "I Still Live." Achsa passed away on July 6, 1862, at the age of thirty-four. A bright and promising child, she was teaching classes at the age of twelve. However, by the age of twenty, she had to give up teaching due to an ailment that left her in severe pain and unable to walk. Achsa was confined to her home and had been bedridden for months. She took to writing poetry in her diary, which described her unfortunate experience: "A young girl in a darkened room, Chained by disease—a living tomb!"

Doctors had a difficult time trying to diagnose the condition Achsa struggled with. Historians believe that she most likely suffered from rheumatoid arthritis. At the age of twenty-six, Achsa claimed she was visited by a spirit that raised her from "a bed of sickness, where I suffered the most extreme pain." She claimed that the spirit told her she would be carried out of the darkness. After her miraculous healing, she traveled the country as a trance medium and became a well-known spiritualist. Achsa wasn't afraid of traveling alone, and her beliefs about the spirit world were strong. At first, she was afraid of speaking, and some of the messages she provided came through automatic writing, a form of channeling spirit messages. She garnered many admirers in her travels, but she never married. When she was traveling, Achsa discovered things in America that she didn't like. The living conditions of the poor who dwelled in the cities and the plight of enslaved people prompted her to speak out. She boldly made statements about women's rights, insisting that opportunities should be equal for both men and women.

Achsa was affectionately called the "the preaching woman," but her travels were eventually cut short when she fell ill again. Some sources say that she knew her time was going to be short, so she continued writing about her thoughts on social justice, freedom, spirits and death. Published reports after her death stated she would continue to communicate through other spiritualist mediums. There were even authors who, after her death, claimed to write her channeled messages. Her grave is one of the most visited at the cemetery, and it has reportedly been this way since her passing. Crystals, stones and folded handwritten notes are some of the mementos people have left behind for this fascinating woman who claimed to travel between the worlds of the living and the dead.

Baird Cemetery

Chittenden, Vermont

Colonel Henry S. Olcott arrived in Chittenden in 1874. He was a serious newspaper reporter who wrote for a newspaper called the *New York Daily Graphic*. He found the perfect family to write about when he arrived: the mysterious mediums and seers of the Eddy family. There was Julia Eddy, who allegedly conversed with those in the spirit world like they were neighbors. Zephaniah, Julia's husband, believed that such abilities were the work of the devil. However, for all of his misgivings about her talents, he invited audiences to come see her and their children's budding psychic skills. Skeptical audiences were particularly cruel to the family, but that didn't stop the show from going on.

Zephaniah and Julia's son Francis Lightfoot Eddy returned home after the Civil War in 1862, fatally ill with consumption. He wrote in the family's Bible the exact hour and day of his death three days before he passed on March 18, 1862. He had told his father that when he died, he wanted his headstone to read "Freedom at Last" with an American flag carved on the stone. The gravestone his father had designed for Francis did not honor his request, and that was said to have enraged his spirit. Allegedly, the spirit of Francis haunted his father until a stone that aligned with his dying request was placed on the grave. That stone can still be found on the grave.

Maranda Eddy, the sister of Francis, also foretold the day of her death. She wanted her stone to be inscribed with: "Not Here But Risen. Why Seek Ye The Living Among the Dead." She died on March 29, 1871. The inscription she requested, as well as the phrase "Entered the World of Spirits" are carved on her gravestone at the Baird Cemetery.

On New Year's Eve 1874, the family opened a "circle room" in their house, which stood near the cemetery. The circle room was designed for spiritual séances and communicating with deceased members of the Eddy family. The crowds that showed up for these experiences were so large that many people had to be turned away. On warm summer nights, people would carry torches and walk the path past the cemetery, up the winding trail to an area known as "Honto's Cave," where apparitions were said to appear during the séances held by brothers William and Horatio Eddy. There are several members of the Eddy family buried at the Baird Cemetery in Chittenden. Did they really know the secrets of life after death?

LAUREL GLEN CEMETERY

Cuttingsville

Along Route 103 in Cuttingsville, Vermont, there is a marble statue of a man who holds a silent vigil at the front door of a spectacular mausoleum at the Laurel Glen Cemetery. In one hand, he holds a skeleton key that is placed over his heart. In his other hand, he holds a pair of gloves and a mourning

Mr. Bowman kneels on the steps of the mausoleum that contains his beloved family.

wreath with a ribbon that reads "for my wife and children." His top hat rests on his arm as he leans forward on one knee toward the entrance. The fine details of his mustache and hair are perfectly rendered. His emotive eyes look into the doorway at a spectacular and heartbreaking temple for the dead. John Porter Bowman was born in his grandparents' tavern at Pierces Corner in Clarendon, Vermont, and his legend tells the story of everlasting love beyond the grave.

John learned about the tanning business growing up, and he ran a successful company called Stony Creek Tanning in New York, which sold leather to the Union army during the Civil War. John married Jennie Gates, who was from Warren, New York, in 1849. Just five years later, the couple lost their first child, Addie, at the age of four months. Ella was the second daughter of the Bowmans, but she died in 1879 at the age of twenty-two. John's wife, Jennie, died six months after the death of their daughter Ella, and John Bowman found himself alone. After suffering that succession of tragedies, John, it was written, became interested in reincarnation. He spent $75,000 building the mausoleum, which was designed to look like a Greek temple. The structure took over a year to build; it consisted of 750 tons of granite and 50 tons of

Left: A close-up of the statue of Mr. Bowman reveals intricately carved details, adding to the lifelike nature of the figure.

Below: Standing behind the statue of Mr. Bowman, one can see his house Laurel Hall across the street.

A view inside the spectacular Bowman Mausoleum.

marble. The work required the skill of over 125 craftsmen. When the work was complete, he had his family interred inside in 1881. A greenhouse was also built on the cemetery grounds so that there were always fresh flowers available to place on the grave of his family. It was recorded that people came from all over the world to see the incredible scene at the cemetery.

Just across the road, around the same time, John commissioned the building of Laurel Hall, a Queen Anne, Victorian–style house, so he could be near his wife and children. It was written that he could look out the windows and from the balconies of the house to see where his family was buried. It was reported that at night, after dinner, he would cross the road to sit with his family. There was speculation that he even held a séance in the house to contact the spirits of his family. In 1891, John Bowman passed away at the age of seventy-five and joined his family in the mausoleum in Laurel Glen. He left a trust of $50,000 in his will to maintain the cemetery and his mansion. The money eventually ran low, and the furnishings of Laurel Hall were sold off to continue maintaining the properties.

The house was rented out to people who maintained that it was haunted by the spirit of Mr. Bowman, which was seen in the house and on the stairs. A business opened in the house in the 1970s, appropriately named the Haunted Mansion Bookshop. The owners of the bookstore were interviewed by the local papers, and they maintained that they never experienced anything ghostly—the tales of hauntings were just legends. There has been debate that after Bowman's death, he hired people to set the dinner table in the house should the family come back from the other side. A statue of his first child was displayed with a light over it at all times. Some accounts say that "wild rumors" abound about Bowman and his properties.

The interior of the Bowman mausoleum is worthy of extensive study for its attention to detail and the symbolism found there. Above the drawers, where the caskets of the Bowman family are interred, "A couch of dreamless sleep" is inscribed, and another inscription in the chamber reads "Sacred to the memory of a sainted wife and daughters." Now-empty candelabras hang from the marble walls. A bust of John Bowman can be seen toward the front of the mausoleum in front of the column. He gazes into the mirror beyond. It is in the mirror that he can see the reflection of his wife and daughter. His infant child, Addie, reaches with outstretched arms toward her father's reflection. Columns of this nature, when carved on gravestones, have symbolized a doorway or entrance into the realm of spirits or spiritual transformation. The entire display is heartfelt and truly depicts a world beyond the veil.

8

SPEAKING STONES

Epitaphs to Remember

Waits the marble in the quarry,
In the mountains rugged breast,
Waits to tell of fame and glory,
Waits to tell where loved ones rest. Some great thought now lies unspoken,
Yet to traverse all the earth;
Silent waits the block of marble
To immortalize its birth.
For our names the marble waiteth; Shall a name for us suffice?
Rather in the hearts that love us Let our monument arise.

—*"The Marble Waiteth," Amanda P. Walker, Grafton, Vermont,*
Poets and Poetry of Vermont *(1860)*

Reaching into the past can sometimes be as simple as brushing away fallen leaves that have gathered in front of gravestones to reveal the carved words that speak to us from long ago. Austin Jacobs Coolidge and John Brainard Mansfield wrote in 1859 in *A History and Description of New England, General and Local*: "Truthful epitaphs are among the most valuable historical records of the lives and times of great men, often presenting volumes condensed into a single line." Later, in 1887, a book documenting the epitaphs in the churchyard of Castleton notes that publishing epitaphs would be a "great service" to the "science of New

Details like the ones depicted on this stone in Bennington lend to the belief that gravestone carving was one of the first forms of folk art in America.

England genealogy." We also learn from this publication that the rhyming verse on many of the gravestones in Castleton was written by Deacon Erastus Higley and Dr. Selah Gridley. Deacon Higley was described as a strong and courageous antislavery man. He outlived six of his seven children.

Gravestone-carvers skillfully carved each letter with precision so that they could be read for as long as the stones could stand the test of time. How does one summarize the life and legacy of someone in just a few lines? Read on to uncover the accomplishments, sorrows and remembrances of those who have gone beyond the veil.

NORTH VERNON CEMETERY

North Vernon, Vermont

Memento Mori [Remember Death]
Here lies, cut down like unripe fruit,
A son of Mr. Amos Tute,
And Mrs. Jemima Tute, his wife—
Called Jonathan, of whose frail life
The days all summed, how short the account, Scarcely to fourteen years
amount.
Born on the twelfth of May was he, In seventeen hundred sixty-three; To
death he fell a helpless prey, April the five and twentieth day,
In seventeen hundred seventy-seven, Quitting this world, we hope, for
heaven.
But tho' his spirit's fled on high.
This body mouldering here must lie; Behold the amazing alteration
Effected by inoculation—
The means employed his life to save Hurried him headlong to the grave.

FAIRVIEW CEMETERY

Norwich, Vermont

*In memory of Mr Nathaniel Hatch who died with the small pox at
Charleston NH July 3ᵈ 1776 aged* [blank]. *His bones were accidentally
found in 1810 by men to work on a turnpike between Charleston and
Walpole and deposited at this place by the desire of his son Oliver Hatch
of this town.
Lest not the dead forgotten
Lest men forget that they must die.*

WEST STREET CEMETERY

Fair Haven, Vermont

*In memory of Ezra Hamilton, who died Feb. 25ᵗʰ, 1810,
In the 77ᵗʰ year of his age.
Farewell, Farewell vain world
Farewell to thee,
For thou hast nothing More to do with me.*

PROSPECT HILL CEMETERY

Brattleboro, Vermont

*The Grave of Alanson D. Wood, who was killed instantly on this river
by the explosion of the Steamboat Greenfield, May 18, 1840. Aet. 30.*

West Brattleboro Cemetery

West Brattleboro, Vermont

Mrs. Susanna Lewis
Wife of Mr. Issac Lewis
Daughr of Mr. Moses Warrener
Died July 27th, 1800
in the 33d year of her age.
To you who now
These lines do see
I pray you would
Remember me.

Staples Cemetery

Danby, Vermont

In Memory of four infants
Of Jacamiah & Mercy Palmer
Was born alive at one birth
& died Nov. 25, 1795.
Four Twen [sic] *infants they are dead And laid in one silent grave*
Christ took small infants in his arms Such infants he will save.

(According to genealogy registers, the children's names were Admirable, Wonderful, Remarkable and Strange.)

Brookside Cemetery

Chester, Vermont

Be it remember'd that this man was a kind & dutiful
Husband, a tender parent, a comfort to his aged parents
Belov'd by his brother'n all tho he had not ariv'd

To middle age yet it pleas'd God that this house of clay
Should not contain him any longer & that he should be
Cloth'd upon by the house eternal in the heavens.
Erected in the memory of Mr. Xenophon Earle
Who died Jan. 25th 1799
In the 29th year of his age
(made by Moses Wright of Rockingham price 17/Dollars)

NORTH MAIN STREET CEMETERY

Rutland, Vermont

In Memory of William T Hall
Who was instantly killed
By the bursting of a cannon
July 4th 1803 in the
32nd year of his age.

(The accident occurred during a Fourth of July celebration.)

PLYMOUTH NOTCH CEMETERY

Plymouth, Vermont

In Memory Of
JOHN TAYLOR
Who, at the age of 16
In this town, made his
Pitch on Black River,
Where he liv'd until
June 11, 1842, then
AE 77 he bid all adieu.

A new country's hardship nor the howl of wild beasts,
Nor wasting disease can disturb thy retreat
Here sweet be thy rest ril Jesus thy King
Shall come & awake thee his praises to sing.

LOCUST RIDGE CEMETERY

Brattleboro, Vermont

In memory of Mr. James Sargeant
Who fell from his waggon in Cambridge-Port
Mass. and was taken-up dead by his
Brother Eli, Dec. 22, 1819 aged 31 years.

In memory of Asa: Son of Mr. David Bemis
And Mrs. Mary his wife: who was
Kill'd with a Log Decr 4ᵗʰ, 1786
Aged 8 years 9m & 9d.

Tho a log crushed his brittle frame
Ye parents praise God's holy Name
Who reigns thru Natures wide Expanse
And not a Sparrow falls by Chance.

CARPENTER CEMETERY

Guilford, Vermont

Sacred to the Memory of the Late
HON BENJAMIN CARPENTER ESQ
Born in Rehoboth, Mass A.D. 1726
A Magistrate in Rhode Island in A.D. 1764
A public teacher of righteousness,
An able advocate to his last for Democracy,
And the equal rights of man.
Removed to this town A.D. 1770
Was a field officer in the Revolutionary War.
A founder of the first constitution and government of Vermont,
A counsellor of Censors in A.D. 1783
A member of the Counsil and Lieutenant
Governor of the state in A.D. 1779
A firm professor of Christianity in the

Baptist church 50 years. Left this world
And 146 persons of lineal posterity
March 29, 1804, aged 78y 10m 12d;
With a strong mind and full faith of a more
Glorious state hereafter. Stature about
6 feet, weight 200. Death had no terror.

CONGREGATIONAL CEMETERY

Castleton, Vermont

Mr. Thomas H. Atwill, a celebrated
Instructor of Sacred Music,
Died Jan. 20, 1814, Aged 50 years.
When friends approach where Atwill sleeps,
No voice, once his, their souls can cheere:
When music charms, then memory weeps,
And mourns for strains that ended here.
'Twas songs divine he sung from choice,
'Tis friendship bids his marble rise:
And friends still hope his heavenly voice
Now sings Redemption in the skies.

Wm. Cullen Died Oct. 11th, 1804;
Aged 16 months. Marcia Died Jan. 25, 1807
aged 21 days. Children of S & B Gridley
Before we ceased to drop a tear,
These infants tombs to view,
Death drop'd his dread commission here,
And seized our Cullen, too!
Life's cruel foe again retn
And aim'd at Marcia's charms,
A weeping mother's fondness spurn'd,
And snatch'd them from her arms.

Prospect Hill Cemetery

Brattleboro

*Bathing in the river near this spot
On the second of July AD MDCCXCVII
Were drowned
Aged seventeen years Pardon Taylor
Son of the Revd Hezekiah Taylor
Of New Fane and
Edward Palmer son of Joseph Pearce Palmer
Of Massachusetts
The former lost his own life
Through generous efforts
To preserve that of his youthful friend.
They were lovely and pleasant in their lives
And in their death were not divided
READER if you knew them
You will weep with their friends!*

Newfane Hill Cemetery

Newfane, Vermont

*Hastings Williams died of a scald
Dec 25th, 1808 in the 3rd year of his age
Son of Capt. William H. & Mrs. Abigail Williams*

*Sudden he fled & left this earthly stage,
Early paid the debt to nature due,
Take solemn warning all of every age,
The King of Terror soon will summon you.*

CONCLUSION

"Vermont"
By Dorothy Canfield Fisher

Wide and shallow in the cowslip marshes Floods the freshet of the April snow.
Late drifts linger in the hemlock gorges, Through the brakes and mosses trickling
slow Where the Mayflower,
Where the painted trillium, leaf and blow. Foliaged deep, the cool midsummer
maples Shade the porches of the long white street; Trailing wide,
Olympian elms lean over
Tiny churches where the highroads meet. Fields of fireflies
Wheel all night like stars among the wheat. Blaze the mountains in the windless
autumn Frost-clear, blue-nooned, apple-ripening days; Faintly fragrant in the
farther valleys
Smoke of many bonfires swells the haze; Fair-bound cattle
Plod with lowing up the meadowy ways.
Roaring snows down-sweeping from the uplands Bury the still valleys,
drift them deep.
Low along the mountain, lake-blue shadows, Sea-blue shadows in the hollows
sleep. High above them
Blinding crystal is the sunlit steep."

Oftentimes, when people think of Vermont, certain images come to mind: vibrant fall foliage, hillside maple syrup shacks, covered bridges and even cheddar cheese. Since researching and

Above: Two slate markers on Route 106 in Reading, Vermont, were carved by a gravestone carver to commemorate an incident of a Native capture of a New Hampshire family.

Left: The family was marched through the area that became Vermont. The birth of the daughter of James Johnson was also noted on one of the stones.

Opposite: A dove representing a peaceful spirit is on the grave of Jenette Russell and a welcoming hand is found on her husband Obadiah in Peru, Vermont.

traveling many roads to write this book, I think of all those aforementioned things, but I also think of so much more. I wish I could express in words the true beauty of the summer sunsets I saw traveling Route 100 that had me yearning for my next trip as soon as I got home to the sea coast. There were so many curious stories I discovered by stopping at roadside signs and historic markers. I even found some markers that looked like gravestones with intriguing carvings and narratives. The gravestone stories and carvings I found in farm fields, at the edge of mossy stone walls and overlooking scenic vistas are part of the Vermont experience, too. Sure, a few places I visited were a little spooky, and I may have looked over my shoulder, just to make sure that the snap of a twig was perhaps a passing chipmunk and not a wandering ghost or spirit. Some graveyards I ventured through provided a very intuitive experience. I just slowly walked toward the areas I just "felt led to," and with each journey, I feel like I got to know the state a little better. So, in some cases throughout this book, I brought you along with me to explore certain stories and, sometimes, an entire cemetery from front to back.

I am so grateful for the many people I met along the way in general stores, at historical societies and in museums who not only helped me with my explorations but encouraged them, too. In that way, you could feel the sense of pride Vermonters still have about their state, which has been present since the very beginning. The care and attention that is needed in many of Vermont's cemeteries is an ongoing process and requires a lot of resources. Not only do the cemeteries risk being reclaimed by the earth underneath them, but there are also incidents of vandalism and even the severe weather that puts gravestones at risk. I read an article in the *Brattleboro Reformer* about a man who was traveling through Bellows Falls in 1923, carrying a load of gravestones, when he recklessly crashed his truck into a tree. Some of these stones were placed in the cemetery with a chip or two in them from the accident. History always has a risk of being forgotten or lost entirely.

> *The stone proved nearly as frail as the lives they marked: storms battered them; tree roots unseated them, lichens colonized them; rodents undermined them; weeds obscured them; vandals overturned them, cows leaned on them, acid rain dissolved them, and frost heaved them.*

—Vermont Magazine, *September 1, 2018*

The gravestones in Vermont each represent a timeline of history that connects us to a path that was traveled before our arrival. The roots of people who were here even before the European settlers arrived are underfoot and deep within Vermont's hills. Explore and honor the past in your travels to the Green Mountain State and if you can help in its preservation. Future generations of cemetery travelers will benefit and thank you.

BIBLIOGRAPHY

Barre Daily Times. "Barn Razed on Site of Fight Naming Barre." June 20, 1936.

Brattleboro Reformer. "He Waited for Death." September 15, 1964.

Burlington Free Press. "Bronze Memorial Statue to John Hubbard Stands Almost Forgotten Over His Grave in Montpelier." April 5, 1968.

———. "Schooner Sunk." July 17, 1907.

———. "Vermont Editorial Opinions." October 5, 1964.

Burlington Weekly Free Press. "Narrow Escape, Shipwreck in Burlington Bay." December 15, 1876.

———. "Right in Our Midst." August 13, 1908, 13.

Bushnell, Mark. "When Medical Students Robbed Graves." *Rutland Daily Herald*, June 26, 2005.

Canfield, Dorothy. *Hillsboro People*. Rahway, NJ: Quinn and Boden Co. Press, 1915.

Collins, Edward Day. *A History of Vermont: With Geological and Geographical Notes, Bibliography, Chronology, Maps, and Illustrations*. United Kingdom: Ginn & Company, 1903.

Currier, John McNab. *Epitaphs of Castleton (Vt.) Church Yard*. Castleton, VT: Town of Castleton, 1887.

———. *Song of Hubbardton Raid*. Rutland, VT: Tuttle and Company, 1880.

"A Farm Town's Haunting Sense of Guilt." *Life* 47, no. 8 (November 2, 1959): 31–34.

Hayes, Lyman Simpson. *The Connecticut River Valley in Southern Vermont and New Hampshire*. Barre: Vermont Historical Society, 1929.

Hayes, Lyman Simpson, and William Danforth Hayes. *The Old Rockingham Meeting House: Erected 1787 and the First Church in Rockingham, Vermont, 1773–1840*. Bellows Falls, VT: P.H. Gobie Press, 1915.

Heller, Paul. "Artists, Anarchists and Christmas Eve in Barre." *Burlington Free Press*, December 19, 1999.

Hemenway, A.M. *The History of the Town of Montpelier for the First One Hundred and Two Years*. Montpelier, VT: Self-published, 1882.

Jones, Doris. "Orville Gibson Murder Still Unsolved." *Rutland Daily Herald*, January 1, 1978.

Journal of American History. Vol. 5. New Haven, CT: Associated Publishers of American Records, 1919.

New England Historical Society. "Another Look at Hetty Green, the Witch of Wall Street." www.newenglandhistoricalsociety.com/another-look-hetty-green-witch-wall-street/.

Newman, Caryn E. "The First American Encyclopedia: Matthew Lyon." Middle Tennessee University. https://www.mtsu.edu/first-amendment/article/1442/matthew-lyon.

Orleans County Monitor. "State News Items." January 30, 1893.

Poets and Poetry of Vermont. Brattleboro, VT: Brown, Taggard & Chase, 1860.

Price, Megan. "Ghost Story." *Rutland Daily Herald*, October 27, 1983.

Rutland Daily Herald. "Bird Mountain." August 30, 1938.

Sauchelli, Liz. "Rotting Tree, Long a Memorial to an Ascutney Farmer, to be Cut Down." *Valley News*, March 12, 2021.

Sessel, Amanda. "Indian Joe Served Vermont Well." *Rutland Daily Herald*, February 22, 1976.

Smith, David W. "The Life of Benjamin Wait." *Waitsfield and Champlain Valley Telecom*, July 2012.

Springfield Reporter. "Springfield Mourns at Last Rites for James Hartness." February 9, 1934.

Times Argus. "Dr. Robert Paddock Barre's First Doctor." July 22, 1970.

Valley News. "Art Notes: Art on the Area's Gravestones." August 13, 2015.

Vermont Journal. "Hetty Green Was a Remarkable Woman." July 14, 1916.

Wells, Frederic Palmer. *History of Barnet, Vermont: From the Outbreak of the French and Indian War to Present Time*. New York: Free Press Printing Company, 1923.

Wilbur, La Fayette. *Early History of Vermont*. Jericho, VT: Roscoe Printing House, 1899.

ABOUT THE AUTHOR

Roxie Zwicker has been entertaining locals, visitors and curious souls with her unique ghost stories since 1994. Her company, New England Curiosities, located in Portsmouth, New Hampshire, has been offering ghost tours and special haunted events since 2002 and is consistently on top of the nation's travel and tourism lists. She has been featured on *Psychic History* on the History Channel and *Destination America* on the Travel Channel and in the *New York Times* and *Boston Globe*. Roxie is the author of eight bestselling books on New England's ghost stories and folklore. Dubbed "Maine's Mystery Maven" by the *York Independent*, Roxie also writes and produces *Wicked Curious*, a podcast based on New England folklore. You can visit her website at www.newenglandcuriosities.com.